Personal Best

A2 Elementary

Student's Book and Workbook combined edition **A**

Series Editor
Jim Scrivener

Student's Book Author
Louis Rogers

Workbook Author
Genevieve White

STUDENT'S BOOK CONTENTS

		LANGUAGE			SKILLS	
		GRAMMAR	PRONUNCIATION	VOCABULARY		
1 You and me		- the verb *be* - possessive adjectives - *'s* for possession	- contractions of *be* - sentence stress	- countries and nationalities - numbers 1 – 1,000 - personal objects	**READING** - a blog about a summer vacation - approaching a text - simple statements with *be*	**SPEAKING** - asking for and giving personal information - asking for clarification **PERSONAL BEST** - a conversation in Lost and Found
1A Meeting and greeting	p4					
1B My summer blog	p6					
1C Is that a "man bag"?	p8					
1D Where's my wallet?	p10					
2 Work and play		- simple present: affirmative and negative - simple present: questions	- *-s* and *-es* endings - auxiliary verbs *do/does* in questions	- jobs and job verbs - activities (1)	**LISTENING** - a video looking at work and free-time activities - listening for names, places, days, and times - introduction to the sound /ə/	**WRITING** - opening and closing an informal e-mail - connectors: *and, but,* and *or* **PERSONAL BEST** - an e-mail to a friend
2A What I do	p12					
2B Weekdays, weekends	p14					
2C Find a roommate	p16					
2D A new city	p18					

1 and 2 REVIEW and PRACTICE p20

3 People in my life		- frequency adverbs and expressions - *love, like, hate, enjoy, don't mind* + noun/*-ing* form	- sentence stress - *-ing* forms	- family - activities (2)	**READING** - a website about local clubs you can join - scanning a text - *also* and *too*	**SPEAKING** - making plans - accepting or declining an invitation **PERSONAL BEST** - making plans with a friend to do an activity
3A Time together	p22					
3B A new group	p24					
3C Opposites attract	p26					
3D A night out	p28					
4 Home and away		- prepositions of time - present continuous	- sentence stress - linking consonants and vowels	- daily routine verbs - the weather and the seasons	**LISTENING** - a video about the weather in different parts of the world - listening for the main idea - sentence stress	**WRITING** - describing a photo - using personal pronouns **PERSONAL BEST** - an e-mail describing a vacation
4A 24 hours in the dark	p30					
4B Weather around the world	p32					
4C A long weekend	p34					
4D A vacation with friends	p36					

3 and 4 REVIEW and PRACTICE p38

5 What are you wearing?		- simple present and present continuous - *can* and *can't*	- dates - *can* and *can't*	- clothes - ordinal numbers - hobbies	**READING** - an article about uniforms and if we like wearing them - identifying facts and opinions - adjectives	**SPEAKING** - shopping for clothes - offering help **PERSONAL BEST** - a conversation in a clothing store
5A Party time	p40					
5B Don't tell me what to wear	p42					
5C Do the things you love	p44					
5D Can I try it on?	p46					
6 Homes and cities		- *there is/there are, some/any* - prepositions of place - modifiers	- *there's/there are* - sentence stress	- rooms and furniture - common adjectives - places in a city	**LISTENING** - a video about unusual homes - identifying key points - contractions	**WRITING** - topic sentences - describing places **PERSONAL BEST** - a description of your town or city
6A A small space	p48					
6B Amazing homes	p50					
6C The Big Apple	p52					
6D Beautiful places	p54					

5 and 6 REVIEW and PRACTICE p56

Grammar practice p112   Vocabulary practice p136   Communication practice p158   Irregular verbs p176

Language App, unit-by-unit grammar and vocabulary games

WORKBOOK CONTENTS

		LANGUAGE		SKILLS	
	GRAMMAR	PRONUNCIATION	VOCABULARY		
1 You and me 1A p2 1B p3 1C p4 1D p5	• the verb *be* • possessive adjectives and *'s* for possession	• contractions of *be* • sentence stress	• numbers 1–1,000, countries and nationalities • personal objects	READING • approaching a text	SPEAKING • asking for and giving personal information
1 REVIEW and PRACTICE p6					
2 Work and play 2A p8 2B p9 2C p10 2D p11	• simple present: affirmative and negative • simple present: questions	• *-s* and *-es* endings • auxiliary *do/does* in questions	• jobs and job verbs • activities (1)	LISTENING • listening for names, places, days and times	WRITING • opening and closing an informal email
2 REVIEW and PRACTICE p12					
3 People in my life 3A p14 3B p15 3C p16 3D p17	• adverbs and frequency expressions • *love, like, hate, enjoy, don't mind* + noun/*-ing* form	• sentence stress • *-ing* forms	• family • activities (2)	READING • scanning a text	SPEAKING • accepting or declining an invitation
3 REVIEW and PRACTICE p18					
4 Home and away 4A p20 4B p21 4C p22 4D p23	• prepositions of time • present continuous	• sentence stress • linking consonant and vowels	• daily routine verbs • the weather and the seasons	LISTENING • listening for the main idea	WRITING • describing a photo
4 REVIEW and PRACTICE p24					
5 What are you wearing? 5A p26 5B p27 5C p28 5D p29	• simple present and present continuous • *can* and *can't*	• dates • *can* and *can't*	• clothes and ordinal numbers • hobbies	READING • identifying facts and opinions	SPEAKING • offering help
5 REVIEW and PRACTICE p30					
6 Homes and cities 6A p32 6B p33 6C p34 6D p35	• *there is/there are, some/any* and prepositions of place • modifiers	• *there's/there are* • sentence stress	• rooms and furniture • common adjectives • places in a city	LISTENING • identifying key points	WRITING • topic sentences
6 REVIEW and PRACTICE p36					

Writing practice p74

UNIT 1 You and me

LANGUAGE the verb *be* ■ countries and nationalities ■ numbers 1–1,000

1A Meeting and greeting

1 What country are you from? Name three more countries near your country.

2 A Match the countries in the box with maps 1–6.

> Colombia   Germany   Turkey   the U.S.   Brazil   Japan

 1 _____
 2 _____
 3 _____
 4 _____
 5 _____
 6 _____

B ▶ 1.1 Listen. Write the letter of each speaker next to the correct map.

3 ▶ 1.1 Listen again. Write the nationality of each country in exercise 2.
the U.S. – American

Go to Vocabulary practice: countries and nationalities, page 136

4 A In pairs, look at the pictures. Where do you think the people are from?

B Read the conversations in exercise 5 and match them with pictures a–c.

a _____

b _____

c _____

5 ▶ 1.3 Listen and complete the conversations.

1
Emilia Hello. My name's Emilia and this is Sara.
Sabine Hi, ⁱ_____ Sabine. Nice to meet you.
Emilia You, too. Where ²_____ from?
Sabine I'm from Germany. And you?
Emilia ³_____ from Colombia, from Bogotá.
Sara I'm not! I'm from Cali.

2
Sam Oscar, this is Meiko. ⁴_____ from Japan. And Meiko, this is Oscar. ⁵_____ from Brazil.
Oscar Nice to meet you, Meiko.
Meiko You, too, Oscar.
Oscar How do you spell your name?
Meiko ⁶_____ M-E-I-K-O.

3
Jo Hi, Ali. How are you?
Ali Good, thanks. And you?
Jo I'm fine. Where are Jean and Paola?
Ali They're not here. ⁷_____ at the conference center.
Jo What about Andreas?
Ali ⁸_____ here. His train's late.

the verb *be* ■ countries and nationalities ■ numbers 1–1,000   LANGUAGE   1A

6 Choose the correct forms of *be*. Use the conversations in exercise 5 to help you. Then read the Grammar box.

'm not   's   're not   'm   're   's not

1 I am = _____
2 You / We / They are = _____
3 He / She is = _____

4 I am not = _____
5 You / We / They are not = _____
6 He / She is not = _____

Grammar   the verb *be*

Affirmative:
I**'m** from Italy.   She**'s** Japanese.   We**'re** German.

Negative:
I**'m not** from Spain.   He**'s not**/He **isn't** here.   They**'re not**/They **aren't** American.

Questions and short answers:
Are you from Spain? Yes, I **am**. No, I**'m not**.   **Is** Andreas here? Yes, he **is**. No, he**'s not**/ he **isn't**.

Go to Grammar practice: the verb *be*, page 112

7 A ▶1.5 **Pronunciation:** contractions of *be* Listen and repeat the contractions.

I'm   you're   he's   she's   it's   we're   they're

B ▶1.6 Say the sentences. Listen, check, and repeat.

1 I'm American and they're Brazilian.
2 He's Irish.
3 You're Peruvian and we're Turkish.
4 She's from Russia.

8 Complete the sentences with the correct form of *be*. Use contractions if possible.

1 Pedro _____ Brazilian. He _____ from Recife.
2 My parents _____ from Poland.
3 Dublin _____ in the UK. It _____ in the Republic of Ireland.
4 "_____ your name Carlos?" "No, it _____ Carlo."
5 "_____ you from Mexico?" "No, I _____. I _____ from Peru."

9 In pairs, look at the pictures. What countries are the people from? What nationality are they?

A This is …   He's American.   **B** No, he's not. He's Canadian!

a   b   c   d   e

Go to Communication practice: Student A page 158, Student B page 167

10 Write the words or numbers.

1 ____ twenty-five
2 36 _____
3 ____ a hundred and forty-three
4 364 _____
5 ____ seventy-seven

6 634 _____
7 ____ two hundred and eight
8 908 _____
9 ____ a thousand
10 894 _____

Go to Vocabulary practice: numbers 1–1,000, page 136

11 In pairs, introduce yourselves to each other. Say your age if you want to.

Hello. My name's …   You, too.   I'm …   I'm … years old.
Nice to meet you.   Where are you from?   How old are you?

Imagine that you meet a famous person. Write the conversation. Introduce yourself and ask him/her about himself/herself.

1 SKILLS READING approaching a text ■ simple statements with *be*

1B My summer blog

1 Do you like sports? What's your national sport? What sports do people usually do in the summer?

> **Skill approaching a text**
>
> Before you read a text, predict as much information as you can.
> - Read the title of the text. Can you guess what it means?
> - Are there any pictures? What people, places, and things can you see?
> - Are there any headings for the different sections? What are the sections about?

2 Read the Skill box. In pairs, look at the title, headings, and pictures in the text. Answer the questions.

1 What type of text is it?
2 Who is the text about?
3 Where is she right now?
4 What is she doing there?

3 Read the text. Choose a title for each post.

1 Week 1   a Time to go home
2 Week 2   b Learning English
3 Week 3   c My host family
4 Week 4   d Enjoying the tournament

4 Read the text again and answer the questions.

1 What is María's nationality?
2 Where are Helen and Alex from?
3 What are María's favorite places in London?
4 Who is Hitoshi?
5 Where is María's English teacher from?
6 Where are the teams in the tournament from?
7 When are the games?

5 Find words in the text to match to the pictures.

1 h_____ f_____

2 c_____

3 t_____

4 g_____

5 c_____

> **Text builder simple statements with *be***
>
> Simple statements with *be* have this pattern: **subject** + **verb** + **complement**:
> **This** **is** my blog.
> **The teams** **are** from Spain, Brazil, Portugal, Poland, Russia, England, Mexico, and Japan.

6 Read the Text builder and look at the Week 1 post in the text again. Draw a box around the subjects, circle the forms of *be*, and underline the complements.

7 In pairs, think of a sport you love. Tell your partner about it.

I love … It's really …

approaching a text ■ simple statements with *be* READING SKILLS 1B

María Gómez
My month in London

Hello! I'm María Gómez. I'm 21 years old, and I'm from Cádiz in Spain. I'm a student, and I love soccer! Right now, I'm in the U.K. I'm at a language school to learn English, but I'm also here for an international soccer tournament for students! This is my blog about my month in London.

Week 1

This is my host family. They're very nice. Helen's English and Alex is Scottish, and their children are named Jenny and Jacob. Jenny's fourteen and Jacob's twelve. Sometimes I play soccer in the park with Jenny and Jacob, and sometimes we all go for a walk in the center of London. It's a really interesting city. My favorite places are Big Ben, Buckingham Palace, and Tower Bridge.

Week 2

This is my language school. There are lots of students from different countries, and we all speak English together. My classmates are really friendly. I always sit with Hitoshi. He's Japanese. Our English lessons are fun! Our teacher's name is Kerry, and she's from Australia.

Week 3

I'm at the soccer tournament now. The teams are from Spain, Brazil, Portugal, Poland, Russia, England, Scotland, and Japan. We train every morning. I think we're a good team because we're very fast. The games are in the evening. They're really exciting!

Week 4

We're the champions! ☺ I'm happy, but I'm also sad because it's the end of my month here. Goodbye, London! Until next time!

Personal Best How many examples of the verb *be* can you find in the text?

7

1 LANGUAGE
possessive adjectives ■ 's for possession ■ personal objects

1C Is that a "man bag"?

1 In pairs, look at the pictures in the text below. Can you name the objects?

2 A Read the text. Do you think the objects in the list are from a handbag, a "man bag", or both?

B ▶1.8 Listen to a radio program. Check (✓) the objects that you hear.

His bag or her bag?

Where do you put your things when you go out? If you're a woman, your things are probably in your handbag, but what about men? Today, 50% of men also have a bag – a "man bag." Is a "man bag" the same as a handbag? And what do men and women carry in their bags?

	HANDBAG	MAN BAG
keys	☐	☐
chewing gum	☐	☐
hairbrush	☐	☐
gloves	☐	☐
candy	☐	☐
tablet	☐	☐
umbrella	☐	☐
phone	☐	☐
wallet	☐	☐
change purse	☐	☐

Go to Vocabulary practice: personal objects, page 137

3 ▶1.11 Listen to the start of the radio program again and choose the correct options.

Host Zoe's here with ¹ *she / her* handbag, and Harry's here with ² *he / his* "man bag." What's in ³ *their / they* bags? Zoe, you first. What's in ⁴ *you / your* handbag?
Zoe Let's take a look. Here are ⁵ *I / my* keys and ⁶ *my / me* hairbrush.

4 A Look at exercise 3 again. Then read the Grammar box. Which possessive adjective is for things that belong to:

1 a man? _____   2 a woman? _____   3 more than one person? _____

B Are possessive adjectives the same or different with singular and plural nouns?

Grammar possessive adjectives

I	my	*my* bag/bags
you	your	*your* umbrella/umbrellas
he	his	*his* pen/pens
she	her	*her* glove/gloves
it	its	*its* photo/photos
we	our	*our* key/keys
they	their	*their* tablet/tablets

Go to Grammar practice: possessive adjectives, page 113

possessive adjectives ■ 's for possession ■ personal objects   LANGUAGE 1C

5 **A** ▶1.13 **Pronunciation:** sentence stress Listen and repeat the sentences. Underline the stressed words in each sentence.
1 What's in your handbag?
2 Here are my keys.
3 His sunglasses are on the table.
4 What's their phone number?

B ▶1.14 Practice saying the sentences. Listen, check, and repeat.
1 Your tablet's new.
2 Where's my umbrella?
3 Here are our photos.
4 Her gloves are blue.

6 Complete the sentences with a subject pronoun or a possessive adjective.
1 My friends are Brazilian. _____'re from Rio de Janeiro.
2 **A** Where are _____ sunglasses?
   B On your head!
3 _____'m Spanish. Here's _____ identity card.
4 _____ name's Ahmed. He's 32 years old.
5 They're from Italy. _____ names are Francesca and Marco.
6 This is George. _____'s from San Diego.
7 We're in the baggage area at the airport, but are _____ bags here?

7 Look at the sentences. Complete the rules about possession. Then read the Grammar box.
1 It's Carl's bag.
2 It's my sister's phone.
3 They're my friends' umbrellas.

After a singular name (e.g., *Mary*), we add ____.
After a singular noun (e.g., *girl*), we add ____.
After a regular plural noun (e.g., *boys*), we add ____.

> **Grammar** **'s for possession**
>
> For a singular noun or name: For a plural noun: Irregular plural nouns:
> Mary**'s** glasses are in her bag. My paren**ts'** car is red. The children**'s** toys are everywhere!

Go to Grammar practice: 's for possession, page 113

8 ▶1.15 Look at the picture and listen to John and Mary. Match the possessions with the people in the box.

John   Mary   John's friends   Mary's sister   Carl

9 Choose the correct options to complete the sentences.
1 It's *Lucy's bag / Lucy bag*.
2 They're *Harry's / Harrys'* glasses.
3 I'm an English teacher. Here are all my *student's / students'* books.
4 It's my *friends' / friend's* phone. Look, this is his photo.
5 Here are the *mens' / men's* umbrellas.

Go to Communication practice:
Student A page 158, Student B page 167

10 A In groups of three to five, follow the instructions.
Student A: Close your eyes.
Other students: Put one of your possessions on the table.
Student A: Open your eyes. Guess whose things are on the table.

Is it Manuel's watch?   *Are they Maria's glasses?*

B Repeat the activity. Take turns being Student A.

Personal Best Think of a person that you know well. Imagine what he/she has in his/her "man bag" or handbag. Say the objects.

1 SKILLS SPEAKING asking for and giving personal information ■ asking for clarification

1D Where's my wallet?

1 Answer the questions below.
1. Look at the picture of a lost property office (Lost and Found) in London. What can you see?
2. What other things can you find in a Lost and Found?
3. What things do you often lose?
4. What buildings usually have a Lost and Found?

2 A ▶ 1.16 Watch or listen to the first part of a webshow called *Learning Curve*. What object is missing?

B ▶ 1.16 Watch or listen again. Check (✓) the things that are in Kate's backpack.

keys □	sunglasses □	cookies □
wallet □	mirror □	tissues □
stamps □	tablet □	chewing gum □

3 ▶ 1.17 Watch or listen to the second part of the show. Are the sentences true (T) or false (F)?
1. The assistant in the Lost and Found is named Harry. ____
2. Kate's personal information is already in the computer. ____
3. Kate loves James Bond. ____
4. Kate's phone is in the assistant's box. ____
5. Simon's phone is different from Kate's. ____

4 A In pairs, complete the questions in the conversation with the words in the box.

address   mobile number   e-mail address   postcode   number   first name   spell

Assistant	Here's the lost property form. Time to fill it out. I'm ready. What's your ¹_____?
Kate	It's Kate.
Assistant	K-A-T-E. What's your surname?
Kate	Oh ... it's McRea.
Assistant	How do you ²_____ that, please?
Kate	M-C-R-E-A.
Assistant	Thanks. And what's your ³_____?
Kate	It's missing.
Assistant	Could you say that again, please?
Kate	My cell phone is lost.

Assistant	OK. Lost mobile. What's your ⁴_____, please?
Kate	It's 02079 46007.
Simon	Isn't that your home phone number?
Kate	Yes, he can call me at home!
Assistant	Could you say that again, please?
Kate	Yes, it's 02079 46007.
Assistant	And what's your ⁵_____, please?
Kate	222 Baker Street, Marylebone, London.
Assistant	OK. What's your ⁶_____?
Kate	NW1 5RT.
Assistant	Do you have an ⁷_____?
Kate	Yes, it's k.mcrea_007@gmail.com.

B ▶ 1.17 Watch or listen again to check.

asking for and giving personal information ■ asking for clarification **SPEAKING** **SKILLS** **1D**

Conversation builder — asking for and giving personal information

Asking for information:
What's your first name/last name (surname)/address/cell-phone number/home phone number/ postal code?
Do you have an e-mail address?
How do you spell that, please?

Saying your phone number:
02079 46007 – oh two oh seven nine four six oh oh seven

Saying your email address:
k.mcrea_007@gmail.com – k dot mcrea underscore oh oh seven at g mail dot com

5 Read the Conversation builder. Answer the questions in pairs.
1 How do you say "0" and "44" in a phone number?
2 How do you say "@," "_," and ".com" in an e-mail address?

6 ▶ 1.17 Read the sentences. Then watch or listen again. Choose the correct options to complete the sentences.
1 The assistant asks Kate to spell her *first name* / *last name* / *address*.
2 He asks her to say her *cell-phone number* / *e-mail address* / *home phone number* again.

Skill — asking for clarification

When you don't understand something, ask the speaker for help:
• Ask him/her to say the sentence again or to spell the word.
• Use **Sorry, could you ...** and **please** to be polite:
  Sorry, could you say that again, please?   *How do you spell that, please?*
• Use polite intonation: *Sorry, could you say that again, please?*

7 ▶ 1.18 Read the Skill box. Listen and repeat the questions when you hear the beeps. Copy the intonation.

8 ▶ 1.19 Listen to three conversations in a school Lost and Found. For what information does the assistant ask for clarification?

Conversation 1   address / postal code / e-mail address
Conversation 2   home phone number / cell-phone number / postal code
Conversation 3   first name / last name / first name and last name

Go to Communication practice: Student A page 158, Student B page 167

9 A **PREPARE** You lose an important personal object. Look at the Conversation builder again. Think about your answers to the questions.

B **PRACTICE** You are at the Lost and Found. In pairs, take turns asking and answering questions and complete the form for your partner. Ask for clarification to check the information is correct.

First name	E-mail address
Last name	Cell-phone number
Address	Home phone number
Postal code	

C **PERSONAL BEST** Exchange with your partner. Read his/her work and correct any mistakes. How could you improve it?

Personal Best Write the e-mail addresses and phone numbers of five people you know. Practice saying them in English.

11

UNIT 2

Work and play

LANGUAGE simple present: affirmative and negative ■ jobs and job verbs

2A What I do

1 Look at the pictures. What jobs can you see?

2 **A** Read the text. Check your answers to exercise 1.

B Label the pictures with the names of the people. What other jobs are mentioned in the text?

My other job

Lots of people around the world have two jobs. Sometimes it's because they need the money, and sometimes they want to learn something new. Let's meet some people who each have two jobs.

1 I'm Luisa. I'm from Brazil, but I live in Lisbon with my parents and my sister. I work as a receptionist for an IT company at an office downtown, but I also help my parents at our family restaurant in the evening and on the weekend. It's a traditional Brazilian restaurant. My sister helps, too. My parents cook the food, and we serve it! I like my two jobs, but I don't have a lot of free time.

2 Michal lives in Prague. He's a mechanic, and he works at a garage. He likes his job because he loves cars, but he doesn't work there on the weekend. On Saturdays, he has a second job – he's a tour guide for tourists. He knows a lot about his city.

3 Zoe's 26 years old and lives in Toronto in Canada. She's a receptionist for a TV company. She works from 9 a.m. to 5 p.m. during the week. Zoe has another job three evenings a week – she teaches Zumba at a gym. She doesn't work on the weekend.

4 Isaac's from Jamaica, but he lives in New York. He's a taxi driver, and he works every day. Isaac likes his job, and he loves New York. He often goes back to Jamaica for his other job. He doesn't drive a taxi in Jamaica – he's a singer, and he sings at festivals!

3 Read the text again. Write the names of the people.

1 They work with cars. _____, _____
2 He/She works with food. _____
3 They have office jobs. _____, _____
4 They come from one country and work in another country. _____, _____
5 They work on the weekend. _____, _____, _____

4 Complete the sentences with verbs from the text.

1 I _____ in Lisbon.
2 My sister _____, too.
3 My parents _____ the food.
4 I _____ a lot of free time.
5 She _____ Zumba at a gym.
6 He _____ a taxi in Jamaica.

Go to Vocabulary practice: jobs and job verbs, page 138

12

simple present: affirmative and negative ■ jobs and job verbs   **LANGUAGE**   **2A**

5 Complete the rules for the simple present. Use the text to help you. Then read the Grammar box.
1 For the *he/she/it* form, we add _____ or _____ to the base form of the verb.
2 For the negative form, we use _____ and _____.

> **Grammar** simple present: affirmative and negative
>
> Affirmative:
> I **work** for an IT company.   He **loves** New York.   She **teaches** Zumba.   My parents **cook** the food.
>
> Negative:
> I **don't have** a lot of free time.   He **doesn't drive** a taxi.

Go to Grammar practice: simple present: affirmative and negative, page 114

6 Complete the text with the correct form of the verbs in parentheses in the simple present.

My parents ¹_____ (have) a hotel in a small town in Spain. I ²_____ (go) to college every day, but I ³_____ (help) my parents in the evening. My dad ⁴_____ (cook) the food, but he ⁵_____ (not serve) it – that's my job. I have two sisters, but they ⁶_____ (not work) in the restaurant. One sister ⁷_____ (live) in Germany, and my other sister ⁸_____ (work) in a hospital.

7 A ▶2.4 **Pronunciation:** *-s and -es endings* Listen and repeat the sounds and verbs in the chart.

/s/	/z/	/ɪz/
likes	goes	finishes

B ▶2.5 Add the verbs to the chart. Listen and check.

teaches   lives   helps   works   drives   watches   makes   sells

8 ▶2.6 In pairs, say the sentences. Listen, check, and repeat.
1 He teaches English.
2 He lives in New York.
3 She helps her parents.
4 He works from 2 p.m. to 10 p.m. every day.
5 He drives a taxi.
6 She watches TV after work.
7 She makes clothes in a factory.
8 She sells books in a store.

9 A Think of three people you know. Write about their jobs, but don't say what the jobs are.

> My friend Ana works in the city. She doesn't work on the weekend. She likes her job because she works with people. She cuts people's hair.

B In pairs, tell each other about your people. Guess the jobs.

A Is Ana a hairdresser?   B Yes, she is. Your turn.

Go to Communication practice: Student A page 159, Student B page 168

10 A Write about your job. Use the prompts to help you.

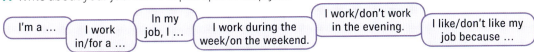

B Work in groups of five or six. Exchange your descriptions with another student. Take turns talking about the person whose description you have. The other students guess who it is.

A This person's a teacher. She works in a language school. She teaches Spanish. She likes her job. She works in the evening, but she doesn't work on the weekend.
B I think Carla's a teacher. Carla, is it you?

Personal Best Write sentences about a dream job.

13

2 | SKILLS | LISTENING | listening for names, places, days, and times ■ activities (1)

2B Weekdays, weekends

1 Match the activities in the box with pictures a–h.

> play tennis   read a book   go to the movies   watch TV
> go for a walk   listen to music   study   meet friends

2 In pairs, talk about the activities in exercise 1. What activities do you do?

I listen to music in the car. I don't go to the movies.

Go to Vocabulary practice: activities (1), page 139

3 ▶ 2.8   Watch or listen to the first part of *Learning Curve*. What do they talk about? Check (✓) the two correct answers.

a free-time activities ☐
b people who enjoy their jobs ☐
c people who don't have any free time ☐

Skill   listening for names, places, days, and times

Names, places, days, and times are important pieces of information when you listen.
- Important words like names, places, days, and times are usually stressed. Listen for stressed words.
- We often use prepositions with places, days, and times: *in* France, *on* Monday, *at* 6:30, etc. Listen for the prepositions *in*, *on*, and *at*.
- Remember to use capital letters for names, places, and days when you write them down.

4 A ▶ 2.8   Read the Skill box. Watch or listen again. Complete the chart with words from the box.

> lawyer   Argentinian   dance teacher   Puerto Rican
> Marcus   English   Maggie   Pablo   tennis coach

Name	Nationality	Job

B In pairs, talk about people you know. Do they love their jobs? Why?/Why not?

My friend Justyna's Polish. She's a receptionist. She likes her job, but she doesn't love it.

listening for names, places, days, and times ■ activities (1) LISTENING SKILLS 2B

5 ▶2.9 Watch or listen to the second part of the show. Complete the sentences with the names and cities in the box.

Toronto   Chip   New York   Gillian   Khan   London

1 This is _____.
   She's from _____.

2 This is _____.
   He lives in _____.

3 This is _____.
   He's from _____.

6 ▶2.9 Watch or listen again. Are the sentences true (T) or false (F)?

1 Gillian meets friends on Saturday. ____
2 She goes running on Monday mornings. ____
3 Khan watches football on Saturday evenings. ____
4 He studies Italian and Spanish. ____
5 Chip starts work at 9 a.m. every day. ____
6 He finishes work at 4 p.m. ____

7 In pairs, talk about the people in the video. Answer the questions.

1 Where do they work?
2 What activities do they do in their free time?
3 What do you think of their jobs?
4 Do you do the same activities in your free time?

Listening builder — introduction to the sound /ə/

The unstressed vowel sound /ə/ is also called "schwa." It is very common in English. We use it in almost every sentence. It is underlined in these phrases:

Marcus isn't a famous tennis player.   What do you do in your free time?   We want to know!

8 ▶2.10 Read the Listening builder. Read the sentences and underline the letters that you think have the sound /ə/. Then listen and check.

1 My sister's a doctor.
2 When do you play tennis?
3 I go to the movies on the weekend.
4 John's a police officer.
5 I want to go out for dinner.

9 A Think of three people that you know. Make notes about the following questions:

• Where do they live? What's their job?
• What activities do they do in their free time? When do they do them?

my friend Victoria – Boston – studies French – Wednesday evenings

B Take turns telling your partner about the people. Listen and complete the chart about your partner's people.

Name	Place	Activity	Day(s)/Time

Personal Best What do you remember about the people in the video? Write a sentence about each person.

2 LANGUAGE simple present: questions

2C Find a roommate

1 Look at the pictures in the text. What do you think "speed-roommating" is?

2 A Read the text and check your answer to exercise 1.

B Look at the questions. Who asks them: people who need a roommate or people who need a room in an apartment?

How to find the perfect roommate

You have a great apartment, and you need a new roommate. How do you find one? Why not try speed-roommating? It's a great way to find the perfect roommate.

The idea for speed-roommating comes from speed-dating. Speed-dating events are for single people who want to find a boyfriend or girlfriend. Speed-roommating is the same idea, but it's for people who need a roommate or a room. You meet new people, talk, and ask questions.

What questions do you ask?

1 Where do you live now?
2 Where's your apartment?
3 What do you do?
4 Are you a neat person?
5 Do you have a boyfriend/girlfriend?
6 Does your boyfriend/girlfriend live near here?
7 Does your apartment have a balcony?
8 What do you do in your free time?

3 A ▶ 2.11 Bruce is at a speed-roommating event. He is looking for a roommate. Listen and decide who is the best roommate for Bruce – Mike, Phil, or Andrea. Why?

B ▶ 2.11 Listen again. Are the sentences true (T) or false (F)?

1 Mike and Bruce work on the weekend. ____
2 Bruce is a DJ at a club. ____
3 Phil doesn't work near Bruce's apartment. ____
4 Phil doesn't like his job. ____
5 Andrea doesn't live with her parents. ____
6 Bruce has a girlfriend. ____

4 Match questions 1–5 with answers a–e.

1 Where do you work?
2 What do you do?
3 Do you work in the evening?
4 Where does your boyfriend live?
5 Do you have a boyfriend/girlfriend?

a He lives in another city.
b I work at a local restaurant.
c No, I don't. Not at the moment.
d I'm an accountant.
e Yes, I do. I finish at about 11:30.

5 A Look at the questions in exercise 4. Which questions have a *yes/no* answer?

B Complete the rule. Then read the Grammar box.
We use the auxiliary verbs ¹_____ and ²_____ to make questions in the simple present.

Grammar   simple present: questions

yes/no questions and short answers:
Do you **work** long hours?   Yes, I **do**.   No, I **don't**.
Does she **go** out?   Yes, she **does**.   No, she **doesn't**.

Wh- questions:
What **do** you **do** in your free time?
Where **do** you **work**?
When **does** he **finish**?

Look! We don't use *do* and *don't* in questions with the verb *be*:
Do you **live** in San Francisco?
Are you from San Francisco?

Go to Grammar practice: simple present: questions, page 115

simple present: questions   LANGUAGE **2C**

6 A ▶ 2.13 **Pronunciation:** auxiliary verbs *do* and *does* in questions Listen to the questions. How do we pronounce *do* and *does*?

1 Do you listen to music?
2 Does Phil have a cat?
3 When do you finish work?
4 What does Bruce do after work?
5 Where do they live?
6 Do they play tennis?

B ▶ 2.13 Listen again and underline the stressed words. Repeat the questions.

7 A Complete the questions asked by different people at a speed-roommating event.

1 _____ you like music?
2 _____ your apartment have two bathrooms?
3 What kinds of TV programs _____ you watch?
4 Where _____ you work?
5 Who _____ you live with?
6 _____ you go out in the evening?

B Ask and answer the questions in pairs.

8 A Do the quiz in pairs. Write down your partner's answers.

B Are you and your partner similar?

What type of **roommate are you?**

1 What time / you / go to bed?
  a 9:00-11:00 b 11:00-01:00 c after 1:00
2 What / you / have for dinner?
  a I cook a healthy meal. b I have a pizza on the sofa. c I go out for dinner.
3 What / do / on the weekend?
  a I relax at home. b I spend time with friends. c I go to parties.
4 How many friends / you / have?
  a 4 or 5 good friends b about 50 c more than 500 on Facebook
5 What / be / your perfect job?
  a a writer b a fashion designer c a rock singer

9 A What do you do in your free time? Ask and answer questions in pairs.

A *What do you do in your free time?*   B *I meet friends, I go out for coffee, and I spend time with my family.*

B Work with a new partner. Ask and answer questions about your first partner.

What does Gabriela do in her free time?

Go to Communication practice: Student A page 159, Student B page 168

10 A Imagine that you want to find a roommate. Write six questions to ask people.

B Go speed-roommating with your classmates. Talk to lots of people. Ask and answer questions. Choose three good roommates.

A *Who do you live with right now?*
B *I live in an apartment with three other people.*

Personal Best Imagine you meet someone at speed-roommating who is a terrible roommate. Write the conversation you have with him/her.

2 SKILLS WRITING — opening and closing an informal e-mail ■ connectors: *and*, *but*, and *or*

2D A new city

1 Think about a town or city that you know well. What do you do there? In pairs, say three sentences to describe the place.

I like Rio de Janeiro. It's a great city. I eat out with my family, I go to the beach, and I go to clubs with my friends.

2 Lucas is in a new city. Read his e-mail to Hayley. Why is he writing? Choose the correct answer.
a to tell her about his new life
b to tell her about his new girlfriend
c to invite her to visit

Hi Hayley,

How are things back home in Australia?

I'm fine here in Singapore. I love life here – it's a fantastic city for students! I share an apartment with two more students near my college. My roommates are named Steve and Susie, and they're great!

I have a part-time job. I work at an Italian restaurant as a waiter. Susie has a job there, too, but I don't work with her because she works on different days. Steve doesn't have a job right now because he goes to college every day.

In the evenings, I study, or I relax and watch TV. I don't have much free time, but sometimes I go to the movies with Steve and Susie. On weekends, I play sports or I go out with my friends. I love the clubs in Singapore!

Write soon.
Lucas

3 Read the e-mail again and answer the questions.
1 Where is Lucas from?
2 Who does he live with?
3 What does he do in Singapore in his free time?
4 What do Lucas and his friends do when they go out?
5 Where does Susie work?
6 Why doesn't Steve work?

Skill opening and closing an informal e-mail

We write informal e-mails to people we know well, like friends and family.

Opening:
Hi/Hello (+ name)   *Hey!*   *Hello!*

Closing:
Write soon.   *Take care.*   *See you soon.*

For very close friends and family, we often close with *Love* + (your name) + the letters *xx*.

4 Read the Skill box. Which opening and closing words or phrases does Lucas use?

opening and closing an informal e-mail ■ connectors: *and*, *but*, and *or* WRITING SKILLS 2D

5 Complete the e-mails with opening and closing phrases.

1 _____ John,
How are you? I hope you're OK.
Are you free on the weekend? Do you want to play tennis on Saturday? I usually play with Victor, but he's in Chicago this weekend.

2 _____

Tom

3 _____ Sara!
How are you? How's your new job?
I'm in a new apartment, and I have two new roommates! The apartment's lovely, and my roommates are really nice.
Do you want to see a movie or go out for coffee on the weekend? I want to hear your news!

4 _____

Nikki xx

Text builder — connectors: *and*, *but*, and *or*

We use *and* to add information:
*My roommates are named Steve and Susie, **and** they're great!*

We use *but* to introduce a different idea:
*I don't have much free time, **but** sometimes I go to the movies.*

We use *or* to add another possibility:
*In the evenings, I study, **or** I relax and watch TV.*

6 Read the Text builder. Find other examples of connectors in Lucas' e-mail.

7 Complete the sentences with *and*, *but*, and *or*.
1 Eduardo's my roommate, _____ he's 22 years old.
2 I like my job, _____ I don't like my boss.
3 On the weekend, I meet my parents at a restaurant, _____ I go to their house for lunch.
4 I play the guitar, _____ I'm not in a band.
5 I have two jobs. I work at a café, _____ I drive a taxi.
6 Does your girlfriend have a job, _____ is she a student?

8 Complete the sentences with your own ideas.
1 Elena's from Colombia, and she …
2 Stefan's from Germany, but he …
3 We often go out on the weekend, and we …
4 In the evenings, we go to the movies, or we …
5 I watch soccer on TV, but I don't watch …
6 In the evening, I …, or I …

9 A PREPARE Plan an e-mail about your life for a friend in another city. Answer the questions.
• Where do you live?
• Who do you live with? Do you like him/her/them?
• Do you have a job? What do you do?
• What do you do in your free time at home? What do you do when you go out?

B PRACTICE Write the e-mail. Use different paragraphs to write about your home, your job, and your free time. Use *and*, *but*, and *or* to connect your ideas.
• Open your e-mail.
• Paragraph 1: Say where you live and who you live with.
• Paragraph 2: Say if you have a job and describe what you do.
• Paragraph 3: Describe what you do in your free time.
• Close your e-mail.

C PERSONAL BEST Exchange e-mails with a partner. Underline three sentences with connectors that you think are interesting.

Personal Best | Describe a city in a different country. Ask your partner to guess the city. | 19

1 and 2 REVIEW and PRACTICE

Grammar

1 Choose the correct options to complete the sentences.

1 _____ in Mexico City.
   a My brother works
   b My brother work
   c My brother has

2 My sister _____ .
   a lives with his parents
   b lives with our parents
   c lives with their parents

3 _____ on the weekend?
   a What does you do
   b What you do
   c What do you do

4 Jack _____ . He's an electrician.
   a 's not construction worker
   b 's not a construction worker
   c no builds

5 How old are you? _____ 25.
   a I
   b I've
   c I'm

6 My hairdresser's Italian. _____ .
   a She comes from Rome
   b They come from Rome
   c She come from Rome

7 _____ American?
   a Your wife's
   b Has your wife
   c Is your wife

8 Who _____ ?
   a do work for
   b do you work for
   c does he works for

2 Put the words in the correct order.

1 apartment New York Harry in Tim and live an in
   _____

2 Canada from 's Harry
   _____

3 a British Tim in 's and bank works
   _____

4 nine He at starts work
   _____

5 restaurant works Harry a in
   _____

6 watch after TV work They
   _____

7 with out On friends the they go weekend
   _____

8 listen and computer games play They music to
   _____

3 Complete the text with the correct form of the verbs in parentheses.

Charles [1] _____ (live) in France, but he works in Switzerland. His wife's German, and they [2] _____ (have) three children. He [3] _____ (be) a lawyer, and she [4] _____ (teach) music. In the evening, she [5] _____ (play) the guitar, and he [6] _____ (fix) watches. On the weekend, they [7] _____ (meet) friends, or [8] _____ (relax) with the family.

Vocabulary

1 Circle the word that is different. Explain your answer.

1 guitar	newspaper	tennis	games
2 doctor	dentist	teach	lawyer
3 Mexico	Irish	Brazil	Peru
4 police officer	Colombian	nurse	teacher
5 Mexican	French	Japan	Italian
6 handbag	keys	gloves	phone
7 sixty	nineteen	seventy	eighty
8 chef	wear	fix	serve

REVIEW and PRACTICE 1 and 2

2 Match definitions 1–8 with objects a–h.

1 They help you see better.
2 They keep your hands warm.
3 It helps you see at night.
4 You keep your money in it.
5 It tells you the time.
6 You use it to send a letter.
7 You use them to open and close a door.
8 You use this on your hair.

a flashlight
b stamp
c glasses
d wallet
e watch
f comb
g keys
h gloves

3 Complete the sentences with the jobs in the box.

chef   dentist   flight attendant   nurse
waiter   mechanic   hairdresser   teacher

1 A _____ serves food in a restaurant.
2 My cousin's a _____ with American Airlines.
3 A _____ cooks the food in a restaurant.
4 A _____ works in a garage and fixes cars.
5 A _____ cuts hair.
6 If you have problems with your teeth, see a _____ .
7 My _____ helps me with my English.
8 My sister's a _____ . She works at a hospital in New York.

4 Put the words in the correct columns.

accountant   gloves   Brazil   Turkish   glasses
sunglasses   Mexican   American   doctor   lawyer
UK   taxi driver   Japan   Irish   tissues   Colombia

Jobs	Countries	Nationalities	Objects

Personal Best

Lesson 1A
Name five nationalities.

Lesson 2A
Name five jobs.

Lesson 1A
Write two sentences about yourself using the verb *be*: one affirmative, one negative.

Lesson 2A
Write three sentences about your friends using the simple present.

Lesson 1B
Write three simple statements with *be*.

Lesson 2C
Write a *yes/no* question using *do* or *does*.

Lesson 1C
Name five things in your bag.

Lesson 2C
Write three questions you can ask the first time you meet someone.

Lesson 1C
Write three sentences using *his*, *her,* and *their*.

Lesson 2D
Give two expressions for closing an informal email.

Lesson 1D
Give two expressions to ask for clarification.

Lesson 2D
Write one sentence with *but* and one with *or*.

21

UNIT 3 People in my life

LANGUAGE frequency adverbs and expressions ■ family

3A Time together

1 When and where do you spend time with your family? Tell your partner.

I see my family on the weekend. We have lunch together on Sundays.

2 Look at the pictures of different family activities. How many generations can you see? What are they doing together?

3 A Read the text. Complete it with the verbs in the box.

go   cook   make   see   play   watch

Family get-togethers

Once a year, my whole family meets at my parents' house for a weekend of fun, music, and great food. We're a big family, and there are four generations of us!

In the morning, we often ¹_____ games with the children in the park. My brother Ben has a boy and a girl. My niece and nephew are crazy about soccer, so we usually play that.

In the afternoon, we ²_____ for a walk or stay at home. We sit in the backyard, and we sometimes ³_____ things with the children. My sister-in-law Lois teaches five-year-olds, and she always brings lots of paper and pens.

In the evening, we ⁴_____ dinner. Food's always an important part of the weekend! Our food's very international – my grandmother's Brazilian, my dad's Colombian, my sister-in-law's British, and my husband's Polish. We often have Mexican food because we all love it.

We never ⁵_____ television – we prefer to talk. My Uncle Paul and my cousins Joe and Megan play music. Uncle Paul and Joe play the guitar, and Megan sings and plays the piano. They're really good.

I don't ⁶_____ my family often because we all live in different parts of the country, but I love these weekends. They're really special.

B ▶ 3.1 Listen and check your answers.

4 A Read the text again and choose the correct options.
1 The writer is Ben's *sister / aunt*.
2 Lois is Ben's *sister / wife*.
3 Paul is Joe's *father / grandfather*.
4 Megan is Paul's *son / daughter*.

B Look at the main picture in the text. What relation to the writer do you think the people are?

Go to Vocabulary practice: family, page 140

22

frequency adverbs and expressions ■ family　　LANGUAGE　3A

5 ▶ 3.4 Listen to Ben and match the activities with the people and the frequency expressions.

1 play tennis	son	every day
2 read stories	grandmother	once a week
3 go out for coffee	son and daughter	once a month
4 watch TV	cousin	three times a week
5 go out for dinner	wife	every evening
6 buy food	brother-in-law	twice a month

6 A <u>Underline</u> the frequency adverbs in the text on page 22. Complete the rule.
Frequency adverbs go *before / after* the verb *be* and *before / after* other verbs.

B Look at the frequency expressions in exercise 5. Which word means "one time"? Which word means "two times"? Then read the Grammar box.

📖 **Grammar** frequency adverbs and expressions

Frequency adverbs:

100%　　　　　　　　　　　　　　　　　　　　　　　　　　　　0%
always　　usually　　often　　sometimes　　hardly ever　　never

Frequency expressions:

once/twice/three times | a / every | day/week/month/year

Go to Grammar practice: frequency adverbs and expressions, page 116

7 A ▶ 3.6 **Pronunciation:** sentence stress Listen to the sentences. <u>Underline</u> the stressed words or syllables. Are the frequency adverbs and expressions stressed?

1 I sometimes play the guitar.
2 He's often late.
3 We never watch television.
4 They eat out once a week.
5 She sees her grandparents three times a year.
6 I listen to the radio every day.

B ▶ 3.6 Listen again and repeat the sentences. Copy the rhythm.

8 A Write five sentences about you and your family. Use different frequency adverbs and expressions.

I often go out for coffee with my mother-in-law.　　*I sometimes watch TV with my grandparents.*
I play soccer with my brother once a week.

B In pairs, say your sentences. Do you do the same activities with the same people?

Go to Communication practice: Student A page 159, Student B page 168

9 A Ask and answer questions with your classmates about how frequently you do the activities.

go to (the movies)　　play (a sport)　　cook　　meet (your cousins)　　drive a car　　go running

A How often do you go to the movies?　　**B** Once a month. What about you?　　**A** I never go to the movies.

B Complete the sentences about your classmates.

1 _____ never goes _____.
2 _____ sometimes plays _____.
3 _____ cooks _____.
4 _____ meets his/her _____.
5 _____ drives a car _____.
6 _____ goes running _____.

Personal Best Draw your family tree. Choose five people in your family and write a sentence about each of them.

3 SKILLS READING scanning a text ■ *also* and *too*

3B A new group

1 Look at the picture. In pairs, talk about how you usually meet new people in your town or city.

Skill scanning a text

Scanning means reading quickly to find specific information; for example, you scan a TV guide for a program, or a schedule for a train's arrival time. You don't read everything. You only look for the information you want.

2 A Read the Skill box. Imagine that you like art and photography. Scan the website to find groups that are suitable for you.

B You are free on Monday and Wednesday evenings. Which art or photography group can you join? Scan the website again.

3 Read the website again and read for detail. Are the sentences true (T) or false (F)?

1 The Walking Club meets on the weekend. ____
2 The Drawing Club always meets in a studio. ____
3 The Italian Club sometimes goes to Italy. ____
4 The Camera Club has an exhibit once a year. ____
5 In the International Friends Club, people cook at different homes every week. ____
6 Children and young people watch the Drama Club's shows. ____
7 The Cooking Club meets once a week. ____
8 The Movie Club always meets every Saturday evening. ____

Text builder *also* and *too*

Also and *too* are adverbs that we use to add extra information. *Also* often goes after the verb *be* and before other verbs. *Too* usually goes at the end of the sentence. We use a comma before *too*, but not before *also*.

4 A Read the Text builder. <u>Underline</u> examples of *also* and *too* on the website.

B Choose the correct words to complete the sentences.
1 She plays the guitar, and she *also* / *too* writes stories.
2 I want to join the Camera Club and the Cooking Club, *also* / *too*.
3 We go to the movies once a month, and we sometimes go to the theater, *also* / *too*.
4 They go to a restaurant twice a week, and they *also* / *too* get takeout once a week.

5 In pairs, discuss which club on the website you like most. Why?

6 A Plan a new club for the website. Think about the following:
What does it do? How often does it meet? Where does it meet?

B Tell the class about your new club and listen to your classmates' clubs. Decide which new club you like most.

scanning a text ■ *also* and *too* **READING** | **SKILLS** | **3B**

Clubs near you

WALKING CLUB

We're a walking club for people who love the country. We go on lots of walks of different lengths and levels of difficulty. We start at 9:30 a.m. on Sunday mornings, and we usually finish at about 5 p.m.

INTERNATIONAL FRIENDS CLUB

We're a friendly group that meets every week on Tuesdays. We usually meet at a restaurant, and we often go to the movies and theater. We want to learn about other countries and cultures, and have a good time, too!

DRAWING CLUB

This is a club for art lovers of all ages. Beginners are very welcome! We don't have a teacher, but we all learn from each other. We work in a studio on Thursday evenings, and we also go outside to draw once a month.

DRAMA CLUB

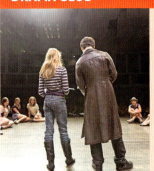

We're a big group, but we always welcome new members. We perform three shows a year at the local arts center and at local schools, too. We meet on Wednesday evenings at 7:30.

ITALIAN CLUB

Buongiorno! We're a group of people who speak Italian and who are interested in Italian culture. We meet at an Italian restaurant once a month, on a Friday evening. We also watch Italian movies together.

COOKING CLUB

We meet every Saturday to cook together at someone's home and then enjoy a great meal! We try lots of new and delicious foods, and we also meet other people who love cooking.

CAMERA CLUB

Do you like photography? If so, come and join our camera club! We meet every Monday at 7 p.m. We have talks and discussions about different kinds of photography, and we show each other our own photos.

MOVIE CLUB

We don't have a regular meeting! Members post a message on the website and invite others to join them for a movie. After watching the movie, we usually go out for coffee and talk. It's a great way to enjoy movies and make new friends, too.

Personal Best — Describe a club that you're in now or when you were a child.

3 LANGUAGE
love, like, hate, enjoy, don't mind + noun/*-ing* form ■ activities (2)

3C Opposites attract

1 Which activities are good for a couple to do together? In pairs, choose five activities and explain why.

> going on vacation   visiting relatives   playing sports   going bike riding
> playing computer games   visiting museums   relaxing at home   studying

Go to Vocabulary practice: activities (2), page 141

2 **A** Read the text about Cara and Chris. What do they do together?

B Discuss the questions in pairs.
1 Are Cara and Chris happy that they are very different? Why/Why not?
2 Do you think opposites attract?

Do opposites really attract? Or is it better to find someone similar to you? We ask one couple why they are together when they are so different from each other.

OPPOSITES attract

CARA
My boyfriend Chris and I are very different. He's always out, and he loves playing sports. He likes running, and he loves playing tennis. I don't mind tennis, but I hate running! I like different activities: I enjoy doing yoga in the park, and I love reading. But I think we're a great couple. Why? We both like living in the city. We enjoy good restaurants, and we love seeing our friends on the weekend, but I sometimes prefer to spend a quiet evening with him at home.

CHRIS
I think it's great that Cara and I have our own interests. I enjoy being active: I play tennis and go running every day. Cara enjoys relaxing at home, and she loves visiting museums and galleries. I don't mind visiting museums, but I hate art! We do some things together – we both love going bowling, for example, but I don't want a girlfriend who's just like me. They say "opposites attract," and I agree!

3 **A** Work in pairs. Read the text again. Student A: write about Cara. Student B: write about Chris. Complete the sentences.

Student A
1 Cara loves _____.
2 She enjoys _____.
3 She likes _____.
4 She doesn't mind _____.
5 She hates _____.

Student B
1 Chris loves _____.
2 He enjoys _____.
3 He likes _____.
4 He doesn't mind _____.
5 He hates _____.

B ▶ 3.8 Tell your partner your answers. Listen and check.

26

love, like, hate, enjoy, don't mind + noun/*-ing* form ■ activities (2) **LANGUAGE 3C**

4 Look at the sentences in exercise 3. Choose the correct option to complete the rule. Then read the Grammar box.

After *love, like, hate, enjoy,* and *don't mind,* we usually use
a a noun or *-ing* form.
b a *to* infinitive.

> **Grammar** *love, like, hate, enjoy, don't mind* + noun/*-ing* form
>
> *love, like,* etc. + noun:
> I *love* TV.
> I *like* books.
> I *enjoy* music.
> I *don't mind* tennis.
> I *hate* museums.
>
> *love, like,* etc. + *-ing* form of verb:
> I *love watching* TV.
> I *like reading* books.
> I *enjoy listening* to music.
> I *don't mind playing* tennis.
> I *hate visiting* museums.

Go to Grammar practice: *love, like, hate, enjoy, don't mind* + noun/*-ing* form, page 117

5 A ▶ 3.10 **Pronunciation:** *-ing* forms Listen and repeat the verbs.

watching   reading   visiting   doing   going   being   playing   running

B ▶ 3.11 Say the sentences. Listen, check, and repeat.
1 I don't mind visiting museums.
2 She doesn't like going bowling.
3 I love reading magazines.
4 He hates going to the gym.
5 We enjoy doing yoga.

6 A Complete Stephanie's profile with the correct form of the verbs in the box.

get   talk   watch   cook   be   play

About me:
Stephanie Ellis

In the evening, I usually make dinner because I don't mind ¹_____. After dinner, I walk my dog Bruno for an hour. It's very relaxing, and I enjoy ²_____ to other dog walkers. I love ³_____ exercise, and sometimes I go running with a friend. I also love ⁴_____ at home with Bruno, but I don't like ⁵_____ TV, and I hate ⁶_____ computer games.

B Look again at the text on page 26. Who do you think is Stephanie's friend: Cara or Chris?

Go to Communication practice: Student A page 159, Student B page 168

7 A Write two true sentences for you for each verb. Use nouns and *-ing* forms.
• I love …
• I like …
• I enjoy …
• I don't mind …
• I don't like …
• I hate …

B Compare your sentences with a partner. Are you similar or different?

A *I enjoy swimming in the sea.*   B *I don't like swimming. I enjoy …*

Personal Best Choose someone you know. Write about what he/she loves, likes, and hates doing.

27

3 SKILLS SPEAKING making plans ■ accepting or declining an invitation

3D A night out

1 A Look at the clocks. Match them with the times.

1 It's ten thirty. ____
2 It's a quarter after ten. ____
3 It's ten o'clock. ____
4 It's twenty-five after ten. ____
5 It's seven minutes after ten. ____
6 It's a quarter to eleven. ____
7 It's five after ten. ____
8 It's twenty after ten. ____
9 It's twenty-five to eleven. ____
10 It's ten to eleven. ____

B ▶ 3.12 Listen and check. Listen again and repeat.

2 ▶ 3.13 Watch or listen to the first part of *Learning Curve*. What's Penny's main problem?

a She is late.
b Ethan is late.
c They don't know what time it is.

3 ▶ 3.13 Watch or listen again. Choose the correct times.

1 Penny's watch says it's five minutes *to/after* ten.
2 The clock on the wall says it's *seven/eleven* minutes after ten.
3 The clock on Penny's computer says it's *a quarter past/half after* ten.
4 Ethan wants to meet Penny at *ten to/ten after* eleven.
5 Ethan's phone says it's ten *thirty/forty*.

4 ▶ 3.14 Watch or listen to the second part of the show and answer the questions.

1 What two activities do they all want to do?
2 What time does Penny arrange to meet Taylor and Ethan?

making plans ■ accepting or declining an invitation **SPEAKING** SKILLS **3D**

Conversation builder | making plans

Suggesting an activity:
Would you like to …?   Do you want to …?   How about having dinner/How about we have dinner …?
Let's go together.   Do you have plans after …?   Are you free for lunch on Thursday?

Agreeing on a time:
What time is good for you?   Let's say 8 p.m.   How about we meet tomorrow at six?
About seven?   Can we go at 8 p.m.?

5 A ▶ 3.14 Read the Conversation builder. Match the two parts to make complete sentences. Watch or listen again and check.

1 What time is   a at five thirty in front of our building?
2 How about we meet   b to come?
3 Do you want to   c seven o'clock?
4 Would you like   d good for you?
5 Are you both free   e for dinner?
6 Can we go at   f go bowling tonight?

B Who says questions 1–6? Write M (Marc), E (Ethan), T (Taylor), or P (Penny). Watch or listen again to check if necessary.

1 ____   3 ____   5 ____
2 ____   4 ____   6 ____

6 In pairs, make plans to see a movie and go shopping together. Take turns suggesting the activity.

Skill | accepting or declining an invitation

When you accept or decline an invitation, it's important to be polite.

- When you accept, be enthusiastic:
  Sure. I like bowling!   *Yes, I'd love to.*   *Cool!*

- When you decline, explain why, and say that you're sorry:
  I'd really love to, but I'm busy tonight.
  Tonight? I'm sorry, I can't. How about another day?

- Use intonation to sound enthusiastic or sorry.

7 A ▶ 3.15 Read the Skill box. Listen to the conversations. Does speaker B accept (✓) or decline (✗) the invitations?

1 A Would you like to go out for dinner tonight?   B ____
2 A Do you want to have a barbecue this weekend?   B ____
3 A How about going swimming tomorrow?   B ____
4 A Do you want to have lunch on Saturday?   B ____

B ▶ 3.15 Listen again. Repeat speaker B's words. Copy his/her intonation.

Go to Communication practice: Student A page 159, Student B page 168

8 A **PREPARE** Think of an activity you want to do with a friend. Use the places in the boxes or your own ideas.

movies   bowling alley   café   restaurant   shopping center   museum   gallery   gym

B **PRACTICE** Invite your partner to do your activity, and accept or decline your partner's invitation politely. Agree on a time and place if you accept.

C **PERSONAL BEST** In groups of four, repeat your conversations, and listen to the other pair. Do they use the phrases from the Conversation builder and Skill box correctly?

Personal Best How often do you go out in the evening during the week? Describe what you normally do.

UNIT 4 Home and away

LANGUAGE prepositions of time ■ daily routine verbs

4A 24 hours in the dark

1 Do you usually do these things in the morning? Discuss in pairs.

> check e-mails   go to the gym   take a bath   take a shower   have breakfast

Go to Vocabulary practice: daily routine verbs, page 142

2 **A** Look at the title of the lesson and the pictures in the text. Which countries sometimes have 24 hours of darkness?

B Read the text. Match the headings in the box with paragraphs A–E.

> Light and dark   Summer activities   Our daily routine   My city   Winter activities

24 hours of night – or day!
by Tom Sanders

A _____
I'm from New York, but I now live in the north of Norway in a small city called Tromsø. I like living here. I have an interesting job, and I like the people.

B _____
I work from 8:00 in the morning to 4:00 in the afternoon. I usually wake up at 6:00 and get up at 6:15. I take a shower and get dressed. At 6:45, I have breakfast and check my e-mails. I leave home at 7:15. My wife and children leave home at 8:00. The children start school at 8:30 and finish at 2:30. I get home at about 5:00.

C _____
Our lives are different in the summer and the winter. In the summer, there are 60 days when the sun doesn't set. From May to July, it's light at midnight. And in the winter, we have 60 days of night. From November to January, it's dark at noon!

D _____
It's very dark, but it's not a bad time of year. On the weekend, we spend time together as a family, or we go skiing. We sometimes see the Northern Lights at night. They're really beautiful.

E _____
In the summer, we spend a lot of time outdoors. In the evening, we often have a barbecue on the beach and, on Friday nights, we sometimes go to outdoor concerts. In July, we go on vacation. We usually visit my family in New York and also spend some time with my wife's family in the mountains.

prepositions of time ■ daily routine verbs | LANGUAGE | **4A**

3 A Read paragraph B again. Cover the text. Ask and answer questions about Tom and his family's daily routine with the verb phrases in the box. What can you remember?

> wake up   have breakfast   leave home   start work/school   finish work/school   get home

A *When does Tom wake up?*   **B** *I think he wakes up at 6:00.*

B In pairs, compare your daily routine with Tom's. What is the same? What is different?

I have breakfast at home, too.   I don't check my e-mails at home.   I get home at six o'clock, not five o'clock.

4 Choose the correct prepositions to complete the sentences. Use the text to help you. Then read the Grammar box.

1 I leave home *at / in* 7:15.
2 *In / From* May *on / to* July, it's light *at / in* midnight.
3 We sometimes see the Northern Lights *in / at* night.
4 *At / In* the summer, we spend a lot of time outdoors.
5 *On / At* Friday nights, we sometimes go to outdoor concerts.

📖 **Grammar**   prepositions of time

in:	on:	at:	from ... to:
the morning(s)	Saturday(s)	5:30	... Monday ... Friday
the winter	Friday night(s)	midnight/noon	... November ... January
July	Monday morning(s)		... 9:00 a.m. ... 5:00 p.m.
	the weekend		

Go to Grammar practice: prepositions of time, page 118

5 A Read about Tom's daughter, Mia. Complete the sentences with the correct prepositions.

1 I usually wake up _____ 5:45 on weekdays.
2 I swim _____ 6:30 _____ 7:30. _____ the weekend, I get up _____ the afternoon!
3 _____ Fridays and Saturdays, I go to bed late.
4 _____ the summer, I often go to concerts _____ night. They don't finish until 2:00 _____ the morning, but it's still light.

B ▶ 4.3   Listen and check your answers. What does Mia love doing? Do you enjoy this activity?

6 ▶ 4.4   **Pronunciation:** sentence stress   Listen and repeat the sentences. Which words are stressed?

1 I get up at six in the morning.
2 I work from Monday to Friday.
3 I go swimming on Wednesday evenings.
4 I walk to work in the summer.
5 My wife gets home at midnight.
6 We have dinner at 8:30.

7 A Complete the sentences so that they are true for you. Write one false sentence.

1 I get up at _____.
2 I work from _____.
3 I _____ evenings.
4 I _____ the summer.
5 I don't _____ the weekend.

B In pairs, say your sentences. Guess the false sentences.

Go to Communication practice: Student A page 160, Student B page 169

8 A Read and answer the questions. Are you a morning person or an evening person?

1 What time do you usually get up on the weekend?
2 What time do you usually go to bed on the weekend?
3 When do you like working or studying?
4 When do you enjoy getting exercise?

B Find a classmate who is like you. Discuss what you like doing in the morning or in the evening. Tell the rest of your class.

David and I are morning people. We like getting up early and going to the gym before work.

Personal Best   Think of someone that you know well. Describe his/her daily routine during the week and on the weekend.

31

4 SKILLS
LISTENING — listening for the main idea ■ sentence stress ■ the weather and the seasons

4B Weather around the world

1 Complete the sentences with the words in the box.

> snowing   hot   cold   raining   cloudy   foggy

1 It's _____.   2 It's _____.   3 It's _____.   4 It's _____.   5 It's _____.   6 It's _____.

Go to Vocabulary practice: the weather and the seasons, page 142

2 A Complete the chart. Then tell your partner about the activities that you do during different seasons.

Season	Months	Weather	My activities

B What is your favorite season? Why? Tell your partner.

Skill   listening for the main idea(s)

It is important to understand the main idea when someone is speaking.
- Use any pictures to help you understand what the topic is.
- Think about who is speaking and what the situation is.
- Don't worry if you don't understand everything. Listen for the important words.

3 ▶ 4.6   Read the Skill box. Watch or listen to the first part of *Learning Curve*. Match places 1–4 with the types of weather a–d.

1 New York   a rainy and very cloudy
2 Mount Emei   b usually warm
3 Bay of Bengal   c very rainy
4 Rome   d sometimes snowy in winter

4 ▶ 4.6   Watch or listen again. For 1–3, check (✓) the correct sentence, a or b.

1
a ☐ It never snows in the fall in New York.
b ☐ Ethan wears his snow boots every day in the winter.
2
a ☐ It rains a lot in Mount Emei, but it rains more in the Bay of Bengal.
b ☐ It's very cloudy in the Bay of Bengal.
3
a ☐ It doesn't often snow in Rome.
b ☐ When it snows in New York, the schools always close.

listening for the main idea ■ sentence stress ■ the weather and the seasons   LISTENING   SKILLS   4B

5 ▶ 4.7 Watch or listen to the second part of the show. For each sentence, write M (Marina), S (Sam), or J (Jenny).

Marina

Sam

Jenny

1 Once in 100 years, there's snow! _____

2 I get about 100 days of sun a year. _____

3 It's like this 200 days a year. _____

4 I love it. Winter is here! _____

5 I sleep early and wake up early. _____

6 We don't usually talk about the weather. _____

6 ▶ 4.7 Watch or listen again. Choose the correct options to complete the sentences.
1 Marina says it's *17°C / −7°C / 18°C*.
2 She goes to her sister's house *after breakfast / in the afternoon / in the evening*.
3 Sam says it's *sometimes / usually / always* hot and sunny in Egypt.
4 His advice is to *wear a hat / wear boots / carry an umbrella* in hot weather.
5 Jenny says the weather forecast is good for *Saturday / Monday / Tuesday*.
6 She *likes / doesn't like / hates* living in Newfoundland.

7 In pairs, think of some advice for visitors to your country for different seasons.
In the winter, it's a good idea to wear warm clothes.

Listening builder | **sentence stress**

In English, we usually stress the most important words in a sentence. These stressed words are usually nouns, verbs, adjectives, and adverbs. You can usually understand the general idea if you only hear these words:
<u>Mount Emei</u> in <u>China</u> gets <u>twenty-seven feet</u> of <u>rain</u> in a <u>year</u>.
In the <u>evening</u>, we have <u>dinner</u> at my <u>sister's house</u>.

8 A Read the Listening builder. Read the text and <u>underline</u> the most important words.

Patagonia is a beautiful part of South America. It's always windy in Patagonia. The wind is sometimes very strong – about a hundred and twenty kilometers an hour. You can't walk when it's so windy.

B ▶ 4.8 Listen and check which words are stressed.

9 Discuss the questions in pairs.
1 Do people in your country talk about the weather a lot?
2 Do you talk about the weather a lot? Who do you talk about it with?
3 What kinds of weather do you like? (sunny weather, rainy weather, etc.)
4 What kinds of weather do you hate?
5 What do people do in your country when the weather is bad?
6 Do you sometimes have strange weather? Describe it.

Personal Best Write a guide to the weather in your country for tourists.

33

4 LANGUAGE present continuous

4C A long weekend

1 What do you like doing when you visit a new city? Tell your partner.

2 **A** In pairs, look at the pictures of Charlotte and Pete's trip. Which city are they in?

B Read Charlotte's posts. Which famous places does she mention?

3 Read the posts again. Answer the questions.
1 Do they like their apartment?
2 What's the weather like?
3 How do they travel around?
4 Do they like the food?

a

We're going away for a long weekend. I'm so excited! We're sitting on the train, and we're waiting to leave for Paris on the Eurostar. I'm having a good time already!

b

We're here. We're staying in a private apartment with a view of the city. It's so romantic!

c

Today, we're visiting the Rodin Museum. We're walking around the beautiful gardens in the warm spring sunshine.

d

Look, it's the Eiffel Tower! I feel like a real tourist. We're having a sandwich and waiting in line.

e

I'm having a good time, but Pete isn't happy. We're going shopping on the Champs-Élysées. He's carrying my bags. I'm feeling hungry – time for lunch.

f

We're at a lovely little restaurant. I'm having the steak! The weather's lovely and warm. What's Pete doing? He's trying to speak French to the waiter.

g

It's late. We're tired, and we're taking a taxi back to the apartment after a great night out. The city lights are amazing!

h

It's our last day. We're buying some food to take home. It's raining, but we don't mind.

4 Match Pete's posts 1–8 with pictures a–h.
1 I'm looking for some French cheese as a present for my mom.
2 The weather's great. We're having a fun time at the museum.
3 We're going to Paris!
4 What a cool apartment! Charlotte's taking a shower, and I'm relaxing after the trip.
5 We're visiting a very famous monument. I want to take a selfie at the top.
6 I'm not enjoying this! I hate shopping!
7 We're going back to the apartment now. Fantastic night out!
8 Finally, I'm sitting down! What's for lunch?

5 **A** Underline the verbs in exercise 4. Which ones describe an action that is happening now?

B Choose *be* or *have* to complete the rule. Then read the Grammar box.

We form the present continuous with the verb *be* / *have* + -ing form.

present continuous LANGUAGE **4C**

Grammar present continuous

Affirmative:
I**'m having** a good time.
He**'s carrying** my bags.
We**'re taking** a taxi home.

Negative:
I**'m not enjoying** this.
It **isn't raining**.

Questions and short answers:
What**'s** Pete **doing**?
Are you **eating** steak?
Yes, I **am**.   No, I**'m not**.

Go to Grammar practice: present continuous, page 119

6 A ▶ 4.10 **Pronunciation:** linking consonants and vowels Listen and repeat the sentences.
I'm getting‿up.   It‿isn't raining.   He's‿eating‿a sandwich.

B ▶ 4.11 Listen and underline the words that are linked. Listen, check, and repeat.
1 What are you talking about?
2 He's enjoying this game.
3 We're sitting in a café.
4 They're going away for a weekend.

7 Complete the dialogues with the present continuous form of the verbs. Then act out the dialogues in pairs.

1 **A** What _____ you _____ (do) here? **B** I _____ (wait) for my friends.
2 **A** _____ it _____ (snow)? **B** No, it _____. It _____ (rain).
3 **A** Why _____ James _____ (wear) a suit? **B** He _____ (go) to a job interview.
4 **A** _____ your friends _____ (leave) now? **B** Yes, they _____. They _____ (look) for their umbrellas.
5 **A** Who _____ Ben _____ (call)? **B** I don't know. He _____ (not / talk) to Alex because Alex is here!

Go to Communication practice: Student A page 160, Student B page 169

8 Work in groups. Take turns miming and guessing the actions.

A *Are you getting dressed?* **B** *No, I'm not.* **A** *Are you taking a shower?* **B** *Yes, I am!*

9 A Charlotte calls her friend, Olivia. Complete the conversation with the correct form of the verbs in the box. Who is Nacho?

visit   have   do   make   play   wait

Olivia   Hi, Charlotte! How are you?
Charlotte Hi, Olivia! I'm good, thanks. I'm in Paris with Pete! We ¹_____ a great time!
Olivia   Paris! That's fantastic. What ²_____ right now?
Charlotte We're at the Eiffel Tower. We ³_____ to go up. Where are you?
Olivia   Nacho and I ⁴_____ my in-laws with the girls. They ⁵_____ in the backyard with Nacho's mom. And Nacho's dad ⁶_____ lunch for us.
Charlotte That sounds nice.

B ▶ 4.12 Listen and check your answers.

10 Imagine you are on vacation. Decide where you are. Call your partner and tell each other where you are, who you are with, and what you are doing.

A *Hello, Ana. It's Daniel.* **B** *Hi! Where are you?* **A** *I'm in New York. I'm going for a walk in Central Park.*

Personal Best Imagine your long weekend. Write eight sentences to describe what you're doing.

35

4 SKILLS WRITING describing a photo ■ using personal pronouns

4D A vacation with friends

1 Ask and answer the questions in pairs.
1 When do you go on vacation?
2 Where do you usually go?
3 Who do you go with?
4 What do you like doing there?

2 A Look at the pictures. Guess where the people are.
B Read the e-mail and check.

Hi Lucy,

[1] How are you? How's work? I hope everything's OK.

[2] I'm in Argentina! I'm visiting Leo and María in Buenos Aires, and I'm having a wonderful time. The weather's amazing! It's 25 degrees, and it's never cloudy. It's hot all day and warm at night. It's so nice after the cold fall weather at home.

[3] Most days I get up early here, and I go running with Leo before breakfast. He loves getting exercise in the morning. Then we return home and have breakfast. Leo and María start work at 8:30, and I leave the apartment with them. I go into the city and visit different places like Casa Rosada and Teatro Colón. In the evening, we go for a walk and then have dinner. The restaurants are great here, and the steaks are fantastic!

[4] I'm sending you a couple of photos that I took. The first photo's of some colorful houses in an area called La Boca. It's a really cool part of town with some amazing buildings. In the second photo, you can see Leo and María. We're having coffee in a local café near their apartment. They have great coffee and delicious pastries there.

My flight's on Friday. See you at work on Monday!

Love, Gemma

3 Read the e-mail again. In which paragraph does Gemma ...
1 write about the weather? _____
2 describe the pictures? _____
3 ask Lucy questions? _____
4 write about her daily routine on vacation? _____

Skill describing a photo

When you send a photo, describe who or what the photo shows. If it shows people, describe what they are doing:
The first photo's of some colorful houses. In the second photo, you can see ...
In this photo, I'm in the park with my friends. We're playing soccer.
This photo's of my sister. She's playing the piano. Here's a photo of our new car.

4 Read the Skill box. Look at Gemma's e-mail again. How does she describe the pictures?

describing a photo ■ using personal pronouns   **WRITING**   **SKILLS**   **4D**

5 A Match the two parts to make complete sentences.

1 In this photo, I'm with
2 Here's a photo
3 In this photo, we're
4 Here's a photo of us in

a Red Square in Moscow!
b fixing our bikes.
c of Sydney at night.
d my niece, Eliza. We're reading a story.

B Match the completed sentences with pictures a–d.

Text builder — using personal pronouns

We often use personal pronouns (*he*, *she*, *it*, etc.) to avoid repeating words and names:
I'm with Sergio and Ana. **We**'re eating fish. **It**'s delicious!
Eleni's helping me with my French homework. **She** speaks really good French.

6 A Read the Text builder. Read paragraphs 3 and 4 in the e-mail again and underline the personal pronouns. What do they refer to?

B Complete the sentences with the correct personal pronouns.

1 I'm with Theo. _____'re waiting for the train.
2 This is the hotel pool. _____'s on top of the hotel.
3 Theo's shopping. _____'s spending all his money!
4 Katie's in bed. _____'s sleeping!
5 The kids are out. _____'re on their bikes.

7 A **PREPARE** Imagine you're on vacation. Decide where you are, what the weather's like, how you're feeling, who is with you, and what to do every day. Imagine two or three photos of your vacation.

B **PRACTICE** Write an e-mail to a friend. Use personal pronouns to avoid repeating words/names.

- Begin your e-mail.
- Paragraph 1: Ask your friend how he/she is.
- Paragraph 2: Describe where you are, what the weather is like, and who is with you.
- Paragraph 3: Describe your daily routine on vacation.
- Paragraph 4: Describe two or three photos of your vacation.
- Finish your e-mail.

C **PERSONAL BEST** Exchange e-mails with a partner. Does his/her e-mail contain personal pronouns to avoid repeating words/names? Can you add any more?

Personal **Best**   Find a photo of people on vacation. Describe their vacation. Where are they? What are they doing?

3 and 4 REVIEW and PRACTICE

Grammar

1 Choose the correct options to complete the sentences.

1 This week _____ in Washington, D.C.
   a I stay
   b I staying
   c I'm staying

2 What _____ right now?
   a do you do
   b are you doing
   c doing you

3 My grandfather always _____ on Sunday afternoons.
   a is visiting
   b visit
   c visits

4 _____ do you see your cousins?
   a How many
   b How often
   c How about

5 My sister's birthday is _____ Friday.
   a at
   b in
   c on

6 My brother's in his room with a friend. _____ computer games.
   a They playing
   b They're playing
   c They play

7 I _____ on the weekend.
   a play always soccer
   b always play soccer
   c play soccer always

8 When _____ go shopping?
   a do you usually
   b usually do you
   c are you

2 Complete the dialogue with the correct form of the verb in parentheses.

A How [1]_____ (be) the new job?
B It's good. Right now, I [2]_____ (work) on a new project.
A Where?
B Near Miami. We [3]_____ (build) a new hotel.
A Where [4]_____ (live) right now?
B I'm living with friends from Monday to Friday, and then I always [5]_____ (come) home on the weekend.
A Are you OK with that?
B I don't mind [6]_____ (travel), and I enjoy [7]_____ (work) on a small team.
A No problems at all?
B Well, I hate [8]_____ (get up) early on Monday mornings!

3 Complete the text with the words in the box.

flies   at   often   arrives   stays
checks   starts   spends

I live in six cities

Barbara Fiala is the owner of Baobab, a communications company, based in New York. She [1]_____ travels for work and spends around two months a year in Europe. She [2]_____ to London and then visits Berlin, Budapest, and Warsaw. She usually [3]_____ three nights in each city and then starts again. She [4]_____ in the evening, so she's ready to work the next day. "I often go for a walk or go to the gym [5]_____ 6 a.m," she says. She [6]_____ work around 7 a.m. and [7]_____ her e-mails and makes some telephone calls before her meetings. In London, she [8]_____ with her sister, but in the other cities she stays in hotels. She does yoga and reads books to relax.

Vocabulary

1 Circle the word that is different. Explain your answer.

1	son	father	niece	brother
2	fall	rain	spring	winter
3	yoga	barbecue	picnic	takeout
4	golf	bowling	volleyball	dancing
5	cold	snowy	warm	icy
6	gallery	museum	gym	violin
7	aunt	grandmother	son	mother
8	karate	swimming	shopping	running

38

REVIEW and PRACTICE 3 and 4

2 Make words to describe the weather.

What's the weather like? It's _____ .

1 d y o c u l _____
2 n d w y i _____
3 t h o _____
4 g y o g f _____
5 m r w a _____
6 y u n s n _____
7 i a n r y _____
8 w g o n n s i _____

3 Put the words in the correct columns.

summer   school   son   swimming   gym   spring
shopping   sister   home   winter   running
uncle   fall   cousin   yoga   museum

Seasons	Relatives	Activities	Places

4 Complete the sentences with the correct form of the verbs in the box.

do   finish   start   walk   get   play   go   have

1 My father _____ up in the morning at six o'clock.
2 He works in a factory and _____ work at 7:30 a.m.
3 I usually _____ to work at 10:00 a.m. on Fridays.
4 To stay in shape, I _____ karate at lunchtime.
5 I _____ work at five in the evening and ride my bike home.
6 In the evening, I _____ my dog for an hour.
7 My sister _____ the violin.
8 We often _____ dinner together.

Personal Best

Lesson 3A Name five relatives.

Lesson 4A Write three things you do every evening.

Lesson 3A Write two sentences using frequency adverbs.

Lesson 4A Think of three time expressions beginning "*In…*".

Lesson 3B Write a sentence using *also*.

Lesson 4C List three things you can do during a weekend in another city.

Lesson 3C Describe two things you like doing, one during the week and one on weekends.

Lesson 4C Write a question and answer using the present continuous.

Lesson 3D Write three times of the day which are important to you.

Lesson 4C Write a negative sentence using the present continuous.

Lesson 3D Give two expressions used for agreeing on a time to meet a friend.

Lesson 4D Describe where you are, what you're doing, and the weather.

39

UNIT 5

What are you wearing?

LANGUAGE simple present and present continuous ■ clothes ■ ordinal numbers

5A Party time

1 Look at the pictures in the text. What are the people wearing? Choose from the words in the box.

> a dress   a shirt   pants   boots   a jacket   sandals   a hat   a suit

Go to Vocabulary practice: clothes, page 143

2 **A** Read the text. Match pictures a–c with names of celebrations 1–3.

B Match sentences 1–5 with the three celebrations.

1 This celebration takes place in Brazil. _____
2 A lot of people wear red for this celebration. _____
3 This celebration starts on a Friday. _____
4 This celebration happens in the winter. _____
5 Animals take part in this celebration. _____

Celebrations
around the world

1 Chinese New Year
My name's Hong, and I live in Shanghai. Today's January 28th, and I'm celebrating Chinese New Year with my family. Chinese New Year always takes place in January or February, but the date changes every year. For example, it's on February 5th in 2019 and on January 25th in 2020. Before New Year, we clean our homes and decorate them in the color red for good luck. Then we have a special dinner with our family and wear red clothes. I'm having dinner with my family now, and I'm wearing a red shirt. We're all having a great time!

2 Rio Carnival
My name's Ana, and I live in Rio de Janeiro. People from all over the world visit Rio at Carnival time. Carnival is on a different date every year, but it's always in February or March. It starts on a Friday and finishes on a Wednesday. Today's Sunday, February 26th – the third day of Carnival – and I'm watching a parade with my friends. The dancers and musicians in the parades are wearing beautiful, colorful costumes.

3 Seville's April Fair
I'm Antonio, and I'm visiting Seville this week for the April Fair. I live in Madrid, but I come to Seville every year in April. Today's April 18th – the second day of the fair – and right now, I'm walking around with my friends. The April Fair is a party for the whole city. It starts at midnight on a Monday and finishes on a Sunday. The women wear flamenco dresses, jewelry, and flowers in their hair, and the men wear suits and hats. Some people ride horses. The atmosphere's fantastic!

simple present and present continuous ■ clothes ■ ordinal numbers   LANGUAGE   5A

3 A Underline the verbs in the simple present and (circle) the verbs in the present continuous in the text.

B Complete the rules with *simple present* or *present continuous*. Then read the Grammar box.
1 We use the _____ to talk about facts and things that happen regularly.
2 We use the _____ to talk about things that are happening now or temporary actions.

Grammar — simple present and present continuous

For things that happen regularly or are always true, we use the simple present:
It always **happens** in January or February.   I **live** in Shanghai.

For things that are happening now or temporary actions, we use the present continuous:
I'**m having** dinner with my family now.   I'**m visiting** Seville this week.

Go to Grammar practice: simple present and present continuous, page 120

4 A Complete the interview with the correct form of the verbs in parentheses. Which person from the text is the interview with?

A Hello. I'm from 103 FM Radio. ¹_____ you _____ a good time? (have)
B Yes, it's amazing! We ²_____ every year. (come)
A What ³_____ you _____ right now? (do)
B We ⁴_____ the local people go by on their horses. (watch) The women look beautiful!
A What ⁵_____ they _____? (wear)
B Long flamenco dresses with special sandals, lots of jewelry, and flowers in their hair. People at the fair always ⁶_____ traditional clothes like that. (wear)
A ⁷_____ you _____ here? (live)
B No, I ⁸_____ just _____ the city this week. (visit) It's my favorite festival in the whole country.
A Great to talk to you! Enjoy the rest of the celebration.

B ▶ 5.3 Listen and check your answers.

Go to Communication practice: Student A page 161, Student B page 170

5 Match festivals 1–5 with dates a–e.
1 New Year's Day   b January 15th
2 U.S. Independence Day   a March 8th
3 Martin Luther King Jr. Day   c January 1st
4 Valentine's Day   d July 4th
5 International Women's Day   e February 14th

Go to Vocabulary practice: ordinal numbers, page 143

6 A ▶ 5.5 **Pronunciation:** dates Listen and repeat the dates. Which words are stressed?

It's July fourteenth.   It's August twenty-fifth.   It's the second of May.   It's the third of June.

B ▶ 5.6 In pairs, say each date in two different ways. Listen, check, and repeat.

It's April first.   It's the first of April.

1 April 1   5 October 31   9 February 26
2 July 4   6 November 20   10 March 5
3 August 8   7 December 30
4 September 12   8 January 16

7 A Ask different classmates about their birthdays. Who has a birthday in the same month as you?

A When's your birthday?   **B** My birthday's on March 7th.
A What do you usually do on your birthday?   **B** I usually go out for lunch with my family. What about you?

B Tell the class about your classmates' birthdays.

Elena's birthday's on June 4th. She always goes out with her friends.

Personal Best   Write sentences about some of your classmates. What do they usually wear to class? What are they wearing today?   41

5 SKILLS READING identifying facts and opinions ■ adjectives

5B Don't tell me what to wear

1 Read the introduction of the text and discuss the questions in pairs.

> **Skill** identifying facts and opinions
>
> Texts often include both facts and opinions.
> A fact is a piece of true information: *New Year's Day is on January 1st*.
> An opinion is what someone thinks about something. You can express an opinion with:
> a verb: *I think (that) …, I don't think (that) …, I agree, I don't agree*
> a positive or negative adjective: *good, fun, fantastic, bad, horrible*

2 **A** Read the Skill box and the text. Find one fact for each person.
   1 Richard _____   4 Nikki _____
   2 Maria _____   5 Hannah _____
   3 Saif _____

   B In pairs, say your facts. Do you remember which person says them?

   A *I wear a uniform on my job – a hat, a shirt, and pants.* **B** *That's Hannah.*

3 Read the text again and answer the questions.
   Which person/people think(s) that …
   1 uniforms aren't for everyone? _____
   2 his/her uniform's not nice? _____
   3 his/her uniform is nice? _____, _____
   4 his/her uniform's not interesting? _____
   5 uniforms are a good idea in his/her situation? _____, _____, _____, _____

> **Text builder** adjectives
>
> Adjectives often show someone's opinion:
> *It's pretty **boring**.*   *We have a **nice** uniform at the bank.*   *The hat's **terrible**.*
> Adjectives come before a noun and after the verb *be*:
> *We wear a **great** uniform.*   *The uniform's **great**!*

4 Read the Text builder. Find more examples of adjectives in the text. Does each one come before a noun or after the verb *be*?

5 Look at the pictures. Imagine you wear one of the uniforms. Write a paragraph about your uniform. Give facts and opinions.

42

identifying facts and opinions ■ adjectives **READING** | SKILLS | 5B

UNIFORMS
ARE YOU A FAN?

Uniforms are common for schoolchildren, police officers, firefighters, soldiers, and a lot of other jobs. But do people like wearing uniforms? Does a uniform make you feel part of a group, or do people dislike looking exactly the same? Here, five readers give us their opinions.

Richard, 16
I wear a uniform to school every day. The uniform for boys is black shoes or sneakers, black pants, a white shirt, and a blue sweater. It's pretty boring, but I don't mind wearing it. I think it's OK to have a school uniform. It means my parents don't need to buy lots of clothes.

Maria, 27
I work in fashion, and clothes are a big part of my life. I always wear fashionable suits to work. It's important to look good on my job – your clothes say a lot about you. Uniforms are fine for some people, but not for me. I don't want someone telling me what to wear.

Saif, 40
Everyone knows we wear a uniform in the fire department. We wear special boots, pants, jackets, gloves, and helmets because we need them. It also shows people that we're firefighters – we're there to help them. I think our uniform's great! It makes me feel part of the fire department.

Nikki, 35
We have a nice uniform at my bank – the women all wear an attractive jacket, a white shirt and scarf, and pants or a skirt. It makes life simple because you don't need to choose your clothes in the morning! I think the uniform's very fashionable, too – it's similar to my own clothes.

Hannah, 21
I wear a uniform on my job – a hat, a shirt, and pants. I don't like my uniform. I don't like the fabric, and the hat's terrible. But I agree that uniforms are necessary on my job because they often get dirty, and I don't want to wear my own clothes at work.

Personal Best — Choose a profession and design an ideal uniform for men and for women. Write a description of it.

5 LANGUAGE   *can* and *can't* ■ hobbies

5C Do the things you love

1 Work in pairs. Match the verbs in the box with pictures 1–5 in the text.

> sew   bake   take photos   paint   make jewelry

Go to Vocabulary practice: hobbies, page 144

2 A Read the Web page. Which people don't have another job?

B Read the Web page again and answer the questions.

1. How does Sandra make money?
2. What does Paul paint?
3. Do people buy Alexa's photos directly from her?
4. Where does Edith sell her clothes?
5. Where do people buy Alain's cakes?

MONEY MONTHLY
Do the things you love

Do you have a hobby? Perhaps you write a blog, collect stamps, or play chess. Or maybe you draw or paint. These are all great hobbies, and many people enjoy doing them for pleasure, but can you make money from your hobby? Read this week's article and find out.

Meet Sandra, Paul, Alexa, Edith, and Alain. They all make money from their hobbies.

1 SANDRA works full time in an office, but in her free time, she makes jewelry. She started making jewelry when she was a girl and now makes earrings, bracelets, and rings, and sells them online. She can earn about $150 a month from her hobby. She also wears some of the things she makes.

2 PAUL's a teacher and, in his free time, he paints. He paints beautiful paintings of animals. People often ask him to paint their pets. He usually goes to their homes to see the pets, draws a picture, and then finishes the painting in his studio at home. He sells about ten paintings every year.

3 ALEXA's a nurse and her hobby is photography. She has three different cameras. She usually visits interesting places on weekends. She takes great photos, and she often uploads her photos to photo libraries. People can't use them for free, but they can pay to download them.

4 EDITH AND ALAIN are retired. Edith can sew and make dresses, shirts, and pants. She sells her clothes at the local market. Alain loves cooking, and he bakes delicious cakes. He sells them to local cafés, and people love them. "It's great," he says. "I can make money simply by doing what I love!"

3 Complete the sentences from the text with the phrases in the box.

> can't use   can pay   can make   can earn

1. She _____ about $150 a month.
2. People _____ them for free.
3. They _____ to download them.
4. I _____ money simply by doing what I love.

can and *can't* ■ hobbies   LANGUAGE **5C**

4 Look at the sentences in exercise 3. Choose the correct options to complete the rules. Then read the Grammar box.

1 We put the base form of a verb *with* / *without* "to" after *can*.
2 The *he* and *she* form of *can* is *the same as* / *different from* the other forms.
3 The negative form of *can* is *can't* / *don't can*.

> **Grammar** *can* and *can't*
>
> *can* to talk about ability:
> He **can** make money by doing what he loves.
> She **can** sew.
>
> *can* to talk about possibility:
> People **can** pay to download them.
> You **can** buy Alain's cake at this bakery.
>
> *can* to talk about permission:
> You **can** park here. We **can** sit here.
>
> Negative:
> People **can't** use them for free.
>
> Questions and short answers:
> **Can** you make money from your hobby?
> Yes, I **can**. No, I **can't**.

Go to Grammar practice: *can* and *can't*, page 121

5 A ▶ 5.9 **Pronunciation:** *can* and *can't* Listen and repeat.

1 My brother can speak Italian.
2 I can ride a bike.
3 My sister can't play the violin.
4 You can't sit there.
5 **A** Can you knit? **B** Yes, I can.
6 **A** Can John play chess? **B** No, he can't.

B ▶ 5.10 Say the sentences. Listen, check, and repeat.

1 I can't swim.
2 You can sell your cakes here.
3 **A** Can I ask you a question? **B** Yes, you can.
4 David can't sew.
5 Ellie can sing.
6 **A** Can you cook French food? **B** No, I can't.

Go to Communication practice: Student A page 161, Student B page 170

6 A Imagine you are the manager of a store. Decide the rules for your salespeople. Complete the sentences with *can* or *can't*.

1 You _____ wear your own clothes at work.
2 You _____ read magazines in the store.
3 You _____ drink coffee and tea when you're at work.
4 You _____ use your phone in the store.
5 You _____ choose what time you have lunch.
6 You _____ get a discount when you buy things in the store.

B In pairs, ask and answer questions about your rules. Do you want to work in your partner's store? Why/Why not?

A *Can I wear my own clothes at work?* **B** *No, you can't. Everyone wears a uniform.*

7 A Match sentences 1–5 with headings a–e.

1 You can't go swimming in the ocean here because we don't have a beach.
2 I can bake really good cookies.
3 You can drive a car if you're over eighteen.
4 You can visit the Science Museum.
5 I can't speak Japanese.

a Your abilities: things that you can do
b Your abilities: things that you can't do
c Things that people can do in your town or city
d Things that people can't do in your town or city
e Things that you can do in your country if you're over eighteen

B Think of more sentences that are true for you in pairs.

In our city, you can watch a soccer game at the national stadium.

Personal Best Write about your favorite hobby. When do you do it? Do you do it with other people? Can you earn money from it?

45

5 SKILLS SPEAKING shopping for clothes ■ offering help

5D Can I try it on?

1 A Do you enjoy shopping for these things? Why/Why not? Tell your partner.

books   food   clothes   shoes   jewelry   sports equipment   birthday presents

B Do you like shopping in these places?

department stores   supermarkets   markets   local stores   online   shopping malls

2 ▶ 5.11 Watch or listen to the first part of *Learning Curve*. Are the sentences true (T) or false (F)?

1 Simon, Kate, and Jack all want some new clothes. ____
2 They have a big event next week. ____
3 They want to order things online. ____

3 ▶ 5.11 Watch or listen again. Choose the correct options to complete the sentences.

1 Simon *likes / loves / doesn't mind* shopping for sports equipment.
2 He *likes / doesn't like / doesn't mind* shopping for birthday presents.
3 He *likes / doesn't like / doesn't mind* shopping at department stores.
4 The big event is a special *dinner / show / party*.
5 "First in Web TV" is a *prize / video channel / website*.

4 ▶ 5.12 Watch or listen to the second part of the show and check (✓) the clothes that Simon, Jack, and Kate try on.

1 coat ☐   6 scarf ☐
2 top ☐   7 shirt ☐
3 skirt ☐   8 dress ☐
4 tie ☐   9 pajamas ☐
5 suit ☐   10 shorts ☐

5 ▶ 5.12 Match the two parts to make complete sentences. Watch or listen again and check.

1 Do you have it   a sell pajamas?
2 What colors   b this credit card here?
3 Do you   c in a size 38?
4 Where are the   d are there?
5 How much   e these on, please?
6 Can I pay with   f is it?
7 Can I try   g women's changing rooms, please?

46

shopping for clothes ◾ offering help **SPEAKING**   SKILLS   **5D**

Conversation builder — shopping for clothes

Asking for information:
Do you have this (suit)/these (jeans) in (blue/a size 38/a medium)?
What colors are there?
Do you sell (pajamas)?
Where are the women's changing/dressing rooms, please?
How much is it/are they?

Asking for permission:
Can I try this (suit) on, please?
Can I pay with cash/by credit card?

this/that/these/those:

I like this (shirt).

I like these (shirts).

I like that (shirt).

I like those (shirts).

6 Read the Conversation builder. Choose two items in the box. In pairs, take turns asking and answering questions about them. Ask about the prices, sizes (small, medium, or large), and colors.

dress   shirt   jacket   jeans   pajamas   shorts

A *Do you have this dress in a small?*   B *No, I'm sorry, we don't. We only have it in a large.*

Skill — offering help

If someone needs something, we can offer to help them:
- Ask if they need help: *Are you all right? Do you need any help?*
- Ask if you can help: *Can I help you?*
- Say what you will do: *Just a minute. I'll check.   I'll show you (where they are). Let me ask someone. I'll be right back.*

7 ▶ 5.13   Read the Skill box. Complete the conversation. Listen and check.
A 1 _____?
B Yes, please. I'm looking for jackets.
A 2 _____.
B Thank you. Do you have this jacket in a large?
A 3 _____. I'll be right back. … Yes. Here you are.
B Thank you very much.

Go to Communication practice: Student A page 161, Student B page 170

8 A PREPARE In pairs, read the situations. Choose your roles. Think about what you need to say.

	Situation 1	Situation 2
Student A	You are a customer. You want to buy a blue T-shirt in a medium. You can spend $20. Ask to try the T-shirt on. Ask about the dressing rooms.	You are a salesclerk in a shoe store. You have shoes in black, brown, and blue, in every size. They are all $40. Offer to help the customer.
Student B	You are a salesclerk in a department store. You have white, blue, and black T-shirts, in small and medium. They are $19.99. Offer to help the customer.	You are a customer. You want to buy some brown shoes in a size 9. Ask about the price. If it's OK, ask to try the shoes on.

B PRACTICE Act out your conversations.

C PERSONAL BEST Find a new partner and act out your conversations again. Is your conversation better this time?

Personal Best Write a conversation between a customer and a salesclerk in a clothing store or department store.

UNIT 6 Homes and cities

LANGUAGE *there is/there are, some/any* ■ prepositions of place ■ rooms and furniture

6A A small space

1 Look at these rooms and items of furniture. Which of them do you have in your home? Can you think of more?

| kitchen   bedroom   living room   stove   closet   armchair   sofa   mirror |

Go to Vocabulary practice: rooms and furniture, page 145

2 A Look at the title of the text and the pictures. How is the apartment special?
  B Read the text and check.

3 Read the text again and answer the questions.
  1 What is Gary's job?
  2 How does Gary make the different "rooms"?
  3 Where is his bed?
  4 Where can guests sleep?
  5 According to the text, what free-time activities can Gary do in the apartment?

24-room micro-apartment

HONG KONG is a busy and exciting city with a population of more than seven million. Like most people in Hong Kong, architect Gary Chang lives in a small apartment. But Gary's apartment has a difference – he can move the walls. It's only 32 square meters, but he can create a lot of new "rooms" inside it.

When you come into the apartment, you see just one room. There's a wall with a TV on it. If you move this, you find a kitchen with a sink and stove. Next to the kitchen, there's a small wall with a washing machine behind it.

Back in the main room, are there any chairs? No, there aren't any armchairs, but there's a small sofa on a wall. You can lift the sofa, pull down the wall, and it becomes a double bed! There are some shelves for books next to the bed, and there's a desk under the shelves.

Another wall in the main room has shelves for Gary's 3,000 CDs. If you move this wall, you find a bathroom behind it. Is there space for visitors? Gary can cover the bathtub to make a bed for guests.

In total, Gary can make 24 different "rooms," including a dining room, a study, and a movie room. There's no balcony, but Gary doesn't mind. He has enough space to have dinner with friends, do yoga, and even have a party!

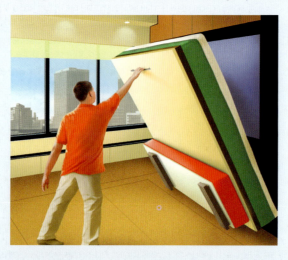 

48

there is/there are, some/any ■ prepositions of place ■ rooms and furniture **LANGUAGE 6A**

4 A Complete the sentences. Check your answers in the text.
1 There _____ a wall with a TV on it.
2 There _____ some shelves for books.
3 There _____ balcony.
4 There _____ any armchairs.

B Choose the correct options to complete the rules. Then read the Grammar box.
We can use *some* and *any* with plural nouns. They mean "more than one."
1 We use *some / any* in affirmative sentences.
2 We use *some / any* in negative sentences and plural questions.

Grammar — there is/there are, some/any

Singular

Affirmative:
There's a TV.
There's an armchair.

Negative:
There's no sofa.
There's no balcony.

Questions:
Is there a washing machine?
Yes, there is. No, there's not. (No, there isn't.)

Plural

Affirmative:
There are some cabinets.

Negative:
There are no/There aren't any stairs.

Questions:
Are there any shelves?
Yes, there are. No, there aren't.

Look! We usually use the contraction *there's* for *there is*. We don't contract *there are*.

Go to Grammar practice: *there is/there are, some/any,* page 122

5 A ▶ 6.4 Pronunciation: *there's/there are* Listen to the sentences and notice how *there's* and *there are* are pronounced. Listen again and repeat.
1 There's a balcony.
2 There are two armchairs.
3 There's no sofa.
4 There aren't any shelves.

B ▶ 6.5 Say the sentences. Listen, check, and repeat.
1 There are five rooms in the apartment.
2 There's a big table in the kitchen.
3 There are no chairs in the living room.
4 There's no garage.

6 A ▶ 6.6 Listen to the description of an apartment. Complete it with the prepositions in the box. Which room is the speaker describing?

behind   in front of   across from   under   next to

This is my favorite room. There's a window ¹_____ the door. There are some chairs and a table ²_____ the window. We have two comfortable armchairs – they're ³_____ the TV, and there's a small table between them. There are some shelves ⁴_____ the armchairs. We have some books and a clock on the shelves. There's a cabinet ⁵_____ the TV.

B Underline two other prepositions of place in the text in exercise 6A. Then read the Grammar box.

Grammar — prepositions of place

We use prepositions of place to say where something or someone is:
Beth's **in** the backyard.   The bathroom's **across from** the bedroom.   Our photos are **on** the shelves.

Go to Grammar practice: prepositions of place, page 122

Go to Communication practice: Student A page 162, Student B page 171

7 Think of a room in your house. What furniture is there? What other objects and possessions are there? Describe it to your partner and ask him/her to draw a plan of it.

Personal Best Write a paragraph about your classroom. Describe what there is.

49

6 SKILLS LISTENING identifying key points ■ contractions ■ common adjectives

6B Amazing homes

1 Match pictures a–h with the adjectives in the box.

| clean   narrow   light   traditional   heavy   wide   modern   dirty |

Go to Vocabulary practice: common adjectives, page 145

2 Think of the homes of your friends and family. Describe them to your partner with the adjectives.

My parents' apartment has a modern kitchen and bathroom. There's an old armchair in the living room.

3 A In pairs, look at the pictures from the show. What adjectives can you use to describe each house?

a house in the Czech Republic   b house in the Philippines

B ▶ 6.9 Watch or listen to the first part of *Learning Curve* and check your answers.

4 ▶ 6.9 Watch or listen again. Which house in exercise 3 do sentences 1–5 describe? Write a or b.

1 This house can move up and down.   ____
2 This house is on an island.   ____
3 This house changes with the weather.   ____
4 This house can get bigger.   ____
5 This house is above the ground because it's dry there. ____

Skill   identifying key points

When people speak, listen for the important things they say.
- Don't worry if you don't understand every word.
- People often give an example of the key points using *for example*, *such as*, or *e.g.*
- Listen to which words are stressed. People often emphasize the most important ideas.

identifying key points ■ contractions ■ common adjectives   **LISTENING**   **SKILLS**   **6B**

5 ▶ 6.10 Read the Skill box. Then watch or listen to the second part of the show. Complete the key points with the names.

1 _____'s home is very big and very old.
2 _____'s home is small, and it's not expensive.
3 _____'s only living in this home for a short time.
4 _____'s home has both modern and traditional things.

6 ▶ 6.10 Watch or listen again. Are the sentences true (T) or false (F)?

1 There aren't any windows in Josh's apartment. ____
2 It's quiet in his apartment at night. ____
3 Charlotte has some new things in her kitchen. ____
4 Her wardrobe's very expensive. ____
5 Danielle's house is in Canada. ____
6 She's cleaning the shelves right now. ____
7 Manu lives in his beach house for nine months every year. ____
8 He's a teacher in California. ____

7 Discuss the questions in pairs.

1 Do you live in a house or an apartment? How old is it?
2 Are there old or new things in it?
3 Describe your favorite room.
4 Do you live in your house or apartment all year?

Listening builder | contractions

When people speak, they usually contract verbs:
He is calling from California! → He**'s** calling from California!
My home is not big. → My home **isn't** big.
I do not understand. → I **don't** understand.

8 A Read the Listening builder. In pairs, complete the sentences from the show with the contractions in the box.

don't   there's   it's   I'm   bed's   they're

1 When _____ cold, the house turns and moves up, and gets a lot of sun.
2 I _____ mean a garage at a house.
3 There are about 300 small apartments. And _____ very cheap.
4 My _____ opposite the kitchen.
5 There are four bedrooms, and _____ a bathroom next to each bedroom.
6 _____ a teacher!

B ▶ 6.11 Listen and check.

9 Discuss the questions in pairs.

1 What do you remember about the homes in the video?
2 Which homes in the video do you like? Why?
3 Which homes don't you like? Why?
4 Do you prefer modern or traditional homes? Why?
5 Do you know someone who lives in an unusual home? Can you describe it?

Personal Best   Write a paragraph about your home or another person's home.

6 LANGUAGE — modifiers ■ places in a city

6C The Big Apple

1 A Think of a city from these continents and regions. Write a fact about each city.

> Europe   Asia   Africa   Latin America   Australasia

B In pairs, tell each other about your cities. Are any of your facts the same?

2 A Look at the pictures. What do you already know about New York City? Make a list in pairs.

B Read the text. What information about New York City is new to you?

So you want to visit …
New York City?

New York — "the Big Apple" — is my favorite city in the world. I love the streets, the modern skyscrapers, and old apartment buildings. It's full of really famous sights, and even on a short visit, you can see a lot of amazing things.

For many people, number one on the list of places to see is the Empire State Building. It's a very famous skyscraper, and there are great views of the city from its 86th and 102nd floors. Another interesting skyscraper is 4 Times Square (formerly the Condé Nast building). It's not beautiful at all, in my opinion, but it's an important "green" building. New York has very cold winters and pretty hot summers, but 4 Times Square produces its own comfortable temperature for most of the year.

For a fantastic view of Manhattan and the Statue of Liberty, visit the Brooklyn Bridge. It's great for taking photos, but it's really busy, with hundreds of cars, bikes, and people. If you get stressed out by the noise, go back to Manhattan and relax in City Hall Park for a while. It's a pretty small park, but it's very special. You can have your lunch there and decide what to do next: see a show on Broadway, go shopping on Fifth Avenue, or go for a walk in Central Park. It's impossible to be bored in this incredible city!

by Harry Fuller

3 Read the text again. What adjectives does the writer use to describe the places?
1 the Empire State Building
2 4 Times Square
3 the Brooklyn Bridge
4 City Hall Park

4 Match sentences 1–5 with pictures a–d. Two sentences match one picture. Then read the Grammar box.
1 This restaurant is very busy.
2 This restaurant's not very busy.
3 This restaurant is pretty busy.
4 This restaurant is really busy.
5 This restaurant's not busy at all.

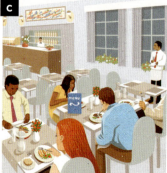

modifiers ■ places in a city   LANGUAGE **6C**

 Grammar modifiers

We use modifiers with adjectives:
There are **really** beautiful views of the city.   It's not a **very** big park.
It's **really** hot in the summer.   It's **not** a beautiful building **at all**.
It's a **pretty** famous building.

Go to Grammar practice: modifiers, page 123

5 Look at the sentences in exercise 4. Rewrite them beginning with *This is*.
This restaurant is very busy. → This is a very busy restaurant.

6 John is staying in a hotel in New York City. Look at his feedback form about the hotel and complete the sentences with *is/isn't* and *very/really* (✓✓), *pretty* (✓), *not very* (X), or *not ... at all* (X X).

In your opinion, this hotel is ...									
comfortable	✓	modern	X	nice	✓	clean	✓✓	expensive	✓✓	quiet	X X

John says that the hotel ...
1 _____ comfortable.   3 _____ modern.   5 _____ nice.
2 _____ clean.   4 _____ expensive.   6 _____ quiet _____.

7 A ▶ 6.13 **Pronunciation:** sentence stress Listen and underline the stressed words in the sentences. Listen, check, and repeat.
1 This is a really interesting city.   4 The café isn't cheap at all.
2 The bridge is pretty wide.   5 Their new house is very traditional.
3 Our office isn't very nice.   6 It's a really famous monument.

B ▶ 6.14 Say the sentences. Listen, check, and repeat.
1 This apartment is really modern.   4 This square is very popular.
2 Pizza Palace isn't a very expensive restaurant. 5 We live in a really old house.
3 Boston is a pretty nice city.   6 This building's not beautiful at all.

Go to Communication practice: Student A page 162, Student B page 171

8 Complete definitions 1–3 with the words in the box.

square   cathedrals   apartment buildings   skyscrapers   mosques   market

1 Religious buildings like _____ and _____ are often very beautiful.
2 _____ are very tall buildings. They can be hotels, office buildings, and _____.
3 A _____ is an open area in a town or city. There's often a _____ there where you can go shopping.

Go to Vocabulary practice: places in a city, page 146

9 A ▶ 6.16 Listen and match the places with the cities.

mosque
square
stadium
market
theater
cathedral
skyscraper

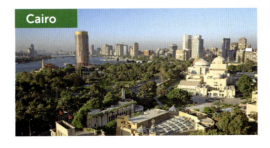
Cairo

Brasília

B ▶ 6.16 Listen again and make notes about the places in Cairo and Brasília. Talk about what you can remember in pairs.
You can buy clothes and jewelry at the market in Cairo.

Personal **Best**   Choose three or four interesting buildings in your city. Write a description of them for a travel website.   53

6 SKILLS WRITING topic sentences ■ describing places

6D Beautiful places

1 A In pairs, match capital cities 1–8 with countries a–h.

1 Kathmandu   a Kenya
2 Wellington   b Poland
3 Lima   c Nepal
4 Warsaw   d Bulgaria
5 San José   e Costa Rica
6 Nairobi   f New Zealand
7 Kingston   g Peru
8 Sofia   h Jamaica

B Think of ten more capital cities.

2 Read the description of Lisbon. Match pictures a–e with paragraphs 1–5.

a _____   b _____   c _____   d _____   e _____

Lisbon a city by the sea

1. Lisbon's the capital city of Portugal. It's on the River Tejo, and it's next to the sea. Lisbon's a pretty small capital city – about 550,000 people live there.

2. Lisbon has some very old areas. Alfama and Graça are beautiful old districts with narrow streets, small squares, and interesting shops. Above them is the castle of São Jorge. There are wonderful views of the city from the castle. You can walk to Alfama and Graça, or you can take the streetcar. It's a great way to see this part of the city.

3. If you want to go on a day trip, take the streetcar to Belém. It's the last district before the beach. There are some interesting museums, a cultural center, and some really beautiful parks. You can try Belém's famous *pastel de nata*, too. These are delicious custard pastries – perfect with coffee.

4. There are lots of places to eat and go out in Lisbon. Bairro Alto's a good place, and there are lots of restaurants and stores. It's pretty noisy at night sometimes. If you want a traditional Portuguese restaurant, go to Alfama or Graça.

5. You can visit Lisbon during any season. It's not very cold in the winter. Spring and fall are lovely times to visit because it's usually warm and sunny. Summer in Lisbon's very hot, but you can go swimming in the sea to cool down!

3 Write the paragraph number for each topic.

1 old parts of Lisbon   ____
2 when to visit   ____
3 geographical information   ____
4 an interesting day trip   ____
5 where to eat and go out   ____

topic sentences ■ describing places **WRITING** **SKILLS** **6D**

🔧 Skill topic sentences

When you write a text, give each paragraph one main topic. The first sentence of the paragraph introduces the topic – we call it a "topic sentence."
For example, in paragraph 1, the "topic sentence" is: *Lisbon's the capital city of Portugal*.

4 A Read the Skill box. Underline the topic sentences in paragraphs 2–5 of the description of Lisbon.
B In pairs, write a topic sentence for each paragraph about Madrid.

1 _____. It's in the middle of the country, and it's on the River Manzanares. Madrid is the capital of Spain and an important political, economic, and cultural center.

2 _____. A really old park is El Capricho. This park has a river, a lake, and some interesting statues and fountains. Another famous park is El Retiro. This is very popular with families.

3 _____. You can go to Plaza de Santa Ana, where there are a lot of fantastic bars and restaurants. Other great areas for going out are La Latina, Malasaña, and Chueca.

🧩 Text builder describing places

Describing a place's location and geography:
… is the capital city of …
… is in the middle of the country/on the River … /next to the ocean.
… people live there.

Recommending places:
There are wonderful views of … from …
If you want to go on a day trip, go to …
… is a good place for …
… is a great way to …
There are lots of places to …

5 Read the Text builder. Complete the sentences about the city of Santiago.
1 Santiago _____ Chile. _____ River Mapocho.
2 _____, go to Pomaire.
3 _____ the city and the mountains from San Cristóbal Hill.
4 Bike riding _____ get to the top of the hill.
5 _____ go out in the evening. Barrio Bellavista _____ restaurants.

6 A **PREPARE** Choose a town or city that you know well. Make notes about the following:
- the location and population
- interesting areas to visit
- places with good views
- places nearby to go on a day trip
- good areas to go out (restaurants, stores, etc.)
- the weather in different seasons

B **PRACTICE** Write a description of your town or city. Begin each paragraph with a topic sentence.
- Paragraph 1: Give geographical information about the location and population.
- Paragraph 2: Describe an interesting area in the city to visit.
- Paragraph 3: Describe a place near the city where people can go on a day trip.
- Paragraph 4: Talk about some good areas to go out.
- Paragraph 5: Talk about the best time to visit.

C **PERSONAL BEST** Read your partner's description. Choose a paragraph that you like. What do you like about it? Is there a topic sentence? Can you improve the paragraph?

Personal Best Write about your favorite area in your town or city. Why do you like it? What can you do there?

5 and 6 REVIEW and PRACTICE

Grammar

1 Choose the correct options to complete the sentences.

1. I usually work in Budapest, but this month _____ in Prague.
   a I work
   b I working
   c I'm working

2. What _____ on the weekend?
   a do you do
   b you do
   c doing you

3. My father _____ speak three languages.
   a can to
   b can
   c is

4. _____ three people in the picture.
   a They're
   b There are
   c There's

5. The letter M is _____ L and N in the alphabet.
   a between
   b behind
   c under

6. I'm sorry, but I _____ come this evening.
   a am not
   b can't
   c don't

7. _____ a good restaurant near here?
   a Is it
   b There's
   c Is there

8. The books are _____ a shelf in the kitchen.
   a at
   b in
   c on

2 Rewrite the sentences with the tense in parentheses.

1. She plays tennis. (present continuous)
   _____
2. They're living in Dubai. (simple present)
   _____
3. What are you doing? (simple present)
   _____
4. We don't work. (present continuous)
   _____
5. Where do you live? (present continuous)
   _____
6. He wears shorts. (present continuous)
   _____
7. She's not listening. (simple present)
   _____
8. Are you playing tennis? (simple present)
   _____

3 Complete the text using the words in the box.

| eat between can't are on in very can |

Inside a luxury plane

This is the Embraer Lineage 1000E. It ¹_____ carry 90 passengers, but this one carries nineteen. There's a living area with leather seats and a wool carpet ²_____ the floor. There ³_____ five TVs and four blu-ray players. The seats turn so four people can ⁴_____ around a dining table. The kitchen has two ovens, an espresso machine, and a $75,000 dishwasher! There's a ⁵_____ large bed ⁶_____ the bedroom and a shower. There are two bathrooms and, ⁷_____ the cockpit and the living area, there's another cabin for the crew. For nineteen passengers, there are two flight attendants and two pilots. For luxury, you ⁸_____ do better than the Embraer Lineage.

Vocabulary

1 Circle the word that is different. Explain your answer.

1	attic	desk	bathroom	kitchen
2	living room	bedroom	kitchen	apartment
3	sew	stove	knit	bake
4	boots	shorts	pants	belt
5	three	second	fourth	first
6	theater	stadium	concert hall	bridge
7	armchair	desk	sofa	chair
8	narrow	heavy	modern	wide

REVIEW and PRACTICE 5 and 6

2 Match definitions 1–8 with nouns a–h.

1. kitchen furniture with a door where you keep things
2. you put books on these
3. shoes for hot weather or the beach
4. bedroom furniture where you keep clothes
5. a building where you can read and borrow books
6. a room under the house
7. earrings, necklace, etc.
8. where you keep the car

a. basement
b. library
c. closet
d. cabinet
e. garage
f. jewelry
g. sandals
h. shelves

3 Put the words in the correct columns.

armchair   jeans   bake   hall   play chess   study
sofa   socks   kitchen   take photos   closet
scarf   bathroom   skirt   knit   bed

Furniture	Hobbies	Clothes	Rooms

4 Complete the sentences with the words in the box.

department stores   bake   jeans   tie
backyard   paint   shorts   monument

1. In my office, all the men wear a _____ .
2. I don't like shopping for _____ . I can never find my size.
3. In the park in our town, there's a _____ made of stone.
4. On the weekend, I love sitting in our _____ .
5. My wife likes to _____ in a modern style.
6. I like local stores, but I hate _____ .
7. In the winter, I _____ bread and cakes.
8. I often wear _____ in the summer.

Personal Best

Lesson 5A — Describe what you're wearing today.

Lesson 6A — Name five rooms in a house.

Lesson 5A — Name five other items of clothing.

Lesson 6A — Write four sentences about your home, with *there's, there's no, there are, there are no*.

Lesson 5C — Name three hobbies with the word *play*.

Lesson 6B — List four pairs of opposite adjectives.

Lesson 5C — List three things you can do well.

Lesson 6C — Name four adjectives to describe cities.

Lesson 5C — Write three sentences about things you can't do in college or at work.

Lesson 6C — Write a sentence with *pretty* or *really*.

Lesson 5D — List three phrases for shopping for clothes.

Lesson 6D — Write three sentences to describe your city.

GRAMMAR PRACTICE

1A The verb *be*

We use the verb *be* to say who people are and to give other information about them (for example, where they are from, what job they do, where they are, how they are).

I'm Juan. I'm Mexican.
This is Michel. He's from France.
My sister is a teacher. She's in the classroom.
How are you? I'm fine.

We also use the verb *be* to talk about ages.

I'm 25.

We add *not* after the verb *be* to make the negative: *'m not*, *'re not*, and *'s not*. We can also use the forms *aren't* for *'re not*, and *isn't* for *'s not*. We form questions by putting the verb before the subject.

The full forms of the verb *be* are *am*, *is*, and *are*. We don't use contractions in short answers.

▶ 1.4	I	he / she / it	you / we / they
+	**I'm** Spanish.	Tom**'s** from Chicago.	You**'re** Japanese.
–	**I'm not** Portuguese.	Maria**'s not / isn't** Australian.	We**'re not / aren't** from Vietnam.
?	**Am** I from Canada?	**Is** she from New York?	**Are** you from Turkey?
Y/N	Yes, I **am**. / No, I**'m not**.	Yes, she **is**. / No, she**'s not / isn't**.	Yes, we **are**. / No, we**'re not / aren't**.

We use the contraction *'s* with third person singular nouns, names, and pronouns.

My sister's here.
Sabine's here.
She's here.

We use the contraction *'re* with *you*, *we*, and *they*.

You're my friend.
We're Colombian.
They're from Brazil.

But we use *are* with plural nouns and names.

My friends are from Brazil.
Gina and Laura are German.

We use the contractions *'s not* or *isn't* with *he*, *she*, and *it*, and *'re not* or *aren't* with *you*, *we*, and *they*.

He's not/He isn't here.
They're not/They aren't here.

We usually use *aren't* with plural nouns and names.

Gina and Laura aren't Brazilian.

1 Complete the sentences with the correct affirmative form of the verb *be*.

1 She _____ Brazilian.
2 They _____ from Argentina.
3 Pedro _____ in the classroom.
4 Fabio and Daniele _____ here.
5 I _____ 27.
6 My name _____ Yara.
7 We _____ students.
8 My teachers _____ American.

2 Read the information. Complete the questions and write the short answers (e.g. *Yes, she is*).

Fiona Murray is a student in Montreal, Canada. She's 22 years old. She's from Boston, in the state of Massachusetts. Her parents are Irish.

1 _____ her name Fiona?
_____
2 _____ she 23 years old?
_____
3 _____ she a student?
_____
4 _____ she from Montreal?
_____
5 _____ her parents Canadian?
_____
6 _____ her parents from Ireland?
_____

3 Complete the conversation. Use contractions where possible.

A Nice to meet you. My name ¹_____ Carla.
B Nice to meet you, too. I ²_____ Chang.
A Where ³_____ you from?
B I ⁴_____ from China. ⁵_____ you from Italy?
A No, I ⁶_____ from Italy. I ⁷_____ from Argentina.
B ⁸_____ you here with your family?
A No, I ⁹_____. They ¹⁰_____ at home.

◀ Go back to page 5

GRAMMAR PRACTICE

1C Possessive adjectives and 's for possession

Possessive adjectives

We use possessive adjectives before nouns to say that something belongs to someone.

It's **my** wallet.
This is **your** book.
This is **her** purse.
Where is **his** bag?
Is this **our** umbrella?
This is **their** car.

🔊 1.12

Subject pronoun	Possessive adjective	
I	my	I'm Spanish. **My** name is Raúl.
you	your	Are **you** ready? **Your** taxi's here.
he	his	**He**'s a great teacher. **His** students are young.
she	her	**She**'s at work, but **her** handbag is at home.
it	its	**It**'s a great city. I like the city for **its** beaches.
we	our	**We**'re from the U.S., but **our** son is British.
they	their	**They**'re not here. **Their** train is late.

We use the same possessive adjective for singular and plural nouns.

It's **my** pen. They're **my** pens.
This is **their** car. These are **their** cars.

's for possession

We add 's to a singular name or noun to say that something belongs to someone.

Tom's book is here.
Where are Lisa's bags?
This is the teacher's desk.

We don't usually use 's to say that something belongs to a thing. We use *of*.

The front of the bus.
The end of the vacation.

With regular plural nouns that end in *-s*, we use an apostrophe (') after the *-s* to talk about possession.

These are the students' books.
My friends' names are Lucy and Samir.

With irregular plural nouns, we use 's to talk about possession.

The children's books are in the classroom.
The women's soccer team are the champions.
Where are the men's bags?

1 Choose the correct words to complete the sentences.
1 *She / Her* is 48.
2 *They / Their* names are Maria and Lucy.
3 *Her / She* keys are in the car.
4 I'm *you / your* teacher for today.
5 *We / Our* tickets are in his wallet.
6 *He / His* is from Vietnam.
7 *I / My* last name is Moszkowski.
8 Is *his / he* umbrella black?

2 Complete the sentences with possessive adjectives.
1 Marie and Sylvain are French. _____ family is from Paris.
2 This is _____ wallet. Look, here's your identity card.
3 I am Chinese. _____ family is from Beijing.
4 Italy is famous for _____ food.
5 _____ classmates are from all over the world. We have interesting discussions in class.
6 She's the mom in my host family. _____ name is Tamara.
7 He's my Spanish friend. _____ name is Marcos.
8 What's _____ last name, Megan?

3 Correct and write the statements and questions. Use 's or an apostrophe (') to indicate possession.
1 Are these your sister glasses?
_____
2 Benedict is Millie boyfriend.
_____
3 My mothers books are in my bag.
_____
4 Our teacher name is Susanna.
_____
5 My parents new car is an Audi.
_____
6 Our children favorite TV show is *The Simpsons*.
_____

◀ Go back to pages 8–9

GRAMMAR PRACTICE

2A Simple present: affirmative and negative

We use the simple present to talk about:

- facts.

I'm Italian.
We live in New York.
He doesn't work at a restaurant.

- regular routines.

I work every day.
We go to the movies on the weekend.
They get up at 10 on Sundays.

We form negatives with *don't/doesn't* + the base form of the verb.

▶ 2.3	I / you / we / they	he / she / it
+	We **work** in a hospital.	Laura **works** in an office.
	I **teach** English.	He **teaches** Japanese.
	They **have** a new car.	She **has** a beautiful apartment.
	You **make** great coffee.	Simon **makes** good tea.
−	We **don't work** in a school.	Paul **doesn't work** in a store.
	I **don't teach** French.	He **doesn't teach** in a school.
	They **don't have** a garden.	She **doesn't have** a dog.
	You **don't love** your job.	Damian **doesn't love** his girlfriend.

We usually add *-s* to the verb to make the third person singular (*he/she/it*) form.

He serves food in the restaurant.
She loves her job.
Ivan sings at festivals.
Camilla helps her parents on the weekend.

Spelling rules for third person singular (he/she/it)

We usually add *-s* to the base form.
work ⇨ works

When the verb ends in a consonant + *y*, we change the *y* to *i* and then we add *-es*.
study ⇨ studies

When the verb ends in *-sh*, *-ch*, *-x* or *-s*, we add *-es*.
finish ⇨ finishes   watch ⇨ watches

Some verbs are irregular.
go ⇨ goes   do ⇨ does   have ⇨ has

1 Choose the correct words to complete the sentences.
1. Adam *have / has* a job in a garage.
2. Dean likes Mexico, but he *don't / doesn't* like Mexico City.
3. Tyler *speak / speaks* French, but he doesn't speak German.
4. Carla works in the evening, but she doesn't *work / works* on the weekend.
5. Barbara and Arnaud *teach / teaches* Spanish at a college.
6. We *doesn't have / don't have* an office in New York.

2 Complete the sentences with the correct affirmative form of the verbs in the box.

| watch   serve   start   cut   help   finish   work |
| go   live |

1. I _____ in an apartment in Rio de Janeiro.
2. He's a waiter. He _____ the food.
3. My sister is a hairdresser. She _____ people's hair.
4. They _____ for a bank in the city.
5. Elena _____ tourists. She gives them information.
6. We _____ to work every morning by bus.
7. Karl _____ TV every evening.
8. Sara _____ work at 9 a.m. and she _____ at 5 p.m.

3 Look at the information and complete the affirmative and negative sentences about Emma.

work: ~~in a hospital~~   in a store
go to work: ~~by bus~~   by car
finish work: ~~at 4 p.m.~~   at 5:30 p.m.
help: ~~tourists~~   customers

1. Emma _____ in a hospital.
   She _____ in a store.
2. She _____ by bus.
   She _____ by car.
3. She _____ at 4 p.m.
   She _____ at 5:30 p.m.
4. She _____ tourists.
   She _____ customers.

◀ Go back to page 13

2C Simple present: questions

We use questions in the simple present to ask about things that are facts, or regular routines. We form questions in the simple present with *do/does* + subject + base form.

Do you like soccer?
Does she live in a big apartment?
Does he work on the weekend?
Do they go out a lot?

We form short answers with *Yes/No*, + subject + *do/does/don't/doesn't*.

Yes, I do.
No, I don't.
Yes, she does.
No, she doesn't

▶ 2.12	I / you / we / they	he / she / it
?	**Do** they **live** in the city?	**Does** he **live** with you?
	Do we **have** more time?	**Does** it **have** a garden?
	Do you **work** at a café?	**Does** she **work** at a hotel?
Y/N	Yes, I **do**. / No, I **don't**.	Yes, she **does**. / No, she **doesn't**.

If we want more information, we put a question word (*what*, *where*, *when*, *why*, *who*, *how*, etc.) before *do/does* at the start of the question.

Where do you live?
Who do you live with?
What does he do on the weekend?
How do you get to work?
When does the class start?
Why do you like soccer?

GRAMMAR PRACTICE

1 Put the words in the correct order to make questions.
1 like / you / do / Spanish / food / ?
_____
2 in / Santiago / does / Sandra / live / ?
_____
3 they / do / Hong Kong / work / in / ?
_____
4 Eric / does / drive / a car / ?
_____
5 finish / do / we / at / 5 p.m. / ?
_____
6 do / teach / English / you / ?
_____

2 Look at the short answers to the questions in exercise 1. Correct the mistakes.
1 Yes, I like. _____
2 Yes, she do. _____
3 No, they not. _____
4 No, he don't drive. _____
5 Yes, we does. _____
6 Yes, I teach. _____

3 Write questions.

1 you / come from Australia
_____
2 your apartment / have / a TV
_____
3 you / like movies
_____
4 when / you / go to work
_____
5 where / your best friend / live
_____
6 what / she / do
_____

◀ Go back to page 17

115

GRAMMAR PRACTICE

3A Frequency adverbs and expressions

We use frequency adverbs with the simple present to talk about routines and how often we do things.

100%
- always — I always watch TV on the weekend.
- usually — I usually read the newspaper on the weekend.
- often — I often go for a walk on the weekend.
- sometimes — I sometimes study English on the weekend.
- hardly ever — I hardly ever drink coffee.
- never — I never watch soccer on the weekend.

0%

We usually put frequency adverbs before the main verb.
I always listen to the radio in the car. NOT ~~Always I listen to the radio in the car~~, or ~~I listen always to the radio in the car~~.

But we put frequency adverbs after the verb *be*.
They're never late. NOT ~~They never are late~~.

We use *How often ... ?* to ask about how frequently actions happen.
How often do you go out for dinner?

We also use frequency expressions with the simple present to talk about regular habits and routines.
I visit my parents every day.
I visit my grandparents twice a week.
I visit my cousins once a year.

▶ 3.5

| I go to the movies | every
once a
twice a
three times a
four times a | day.
week.
month.
year. |

Once means "one time" and *twice* means "two times."

We usually use frequency expressions at the end of a sentence. We sometimes use them at the start of a sentence.
I visit my cousins once a year.
Once a year, I visit my cousins.
NOT ~~I once a year visit my cousins~~.

1. Rewrite the sentences. Put the frequency adverbs in the correct places.
   1. My father reads the newspaper. (always)
   2. My aunt has lunch with friends. (often)
   3. My cousin is at home in the evening. (usually)
   4. They work on the weekend. (sometimes)
   5. I go to the movies. (never)
   6. I'm very busy. (often)

2. Complete the sentences. Put one word in each sentence.

   1. I go to the gym _____ day.
   2. We go on vacation three times a _____ – in March, May, and October.
   3. I see my grandparents twice _____ week.
   4. I usually have a cup of coffee _____ a day – with breakfast and after lunch.
   5. My dad plays golf three _____ a week.
   6. My brother visits me twice a week, but my sister only visits me _____ a week.

3. Correct the sentences.
   1. Never Sam listens to music.
   2. Always the apartments here are nice.
   3. We eat out hardly ever on Saturdays.
   4. Lidia drives to work every days.
   5. We see our cousins four or five times year.
   6. I go to the theater once time a month.

◀ Go back to page 23

116

GRAMMAR PRACTICE

3C love, like, hate, enjoy, don't mind + noun/-ing form

We use *love*, *like*, *hate*, *enjoy*, and *don't mind* to say if we feel positively or negatively about something.

The verbs *love*, *like*, and *enjoy* have a positive meaning.

I love tennis. ☺☺
I like basketball. ☺
I enjoy swimming. ☺

The verb *don't mind* has a neutral meaning.

I don't mind working on the weekend. 😐
Soraya doesn't mind cats. 😐

The verbs *don't like/don't enjoy* and *hate* have a negative meaning.

I don't like going to the gym. ☹
Emil hates watching soccer. ☹☹

We use a noun or the *-ing* form of a verb after these verbs. (We can also use the infinitive after *love*, *like*, and *hate*.)

▶ 3.9

I love	tennis. / playing tennis.
I enjoy	museums. / visiting museums.
I like	dogs. / walking my dog.
I don't mind	rock music. / listening to rock music.
I don't like	Indian food. / eating Indian food.
I hate	soccer. / watching soccer.

Spelling rules for the *-ing* form

We usually add *-ing* to the base form of the verb.

play ⇨ playing   talk ⇨ talking

When a verb ends in consonant + *e*, we usually remove the *e* and then add *-ing*.

take ⇨ taking   live ⇨ living
BUT be ⇨ being

When a one-syllable verb ends in a vowel + a consonant, we double the consonant and then add *-ing*.

sit ⇨ sitting   plan ⇨ planning

When a one-syllable verb ends in a vowel + a consonant, we double the consonant and then add *-ing*.

sit ⇨ sitting   plan ⇨ planning

1 Complete the sentences with the *-ing* form of the verb in parentheses.
  1 They like _____ new places. (visit)
  2 I like _____ time with my family. (spend)
  3 He doesn't like _____. (swim)
  4 She hates _____ dinner. (make)
  5 Does Freya like _____? (drive)
  6 I love _____ on the beach. (run)
  7 Do you like _____ a student? (be)
  8 My parents love _____ photos. (take)

2 Complete the sentences with *love*, *like*, *don't mind*, *don't like*, *hate*, and the *-ing* form of the verbs in the box.

   | work go meet play make cook learn listen |

  1 They ☺ _____ Japanese food.
  2 Sadiq ☺ _____ in a bank.
  3 I ☹ _____ French.
  4 Tania ☺☺ _____ clothes.
  5 I ☺ _____ my friends in town.
  6 We ☹☹ _____ golf.
  7 Liam 😐 _____ shopping.
  8 I ☺ _____ to the radio.

3 Read the sentences. Check (✔) the ones that are correct. Rewrite the incorrect ones.
  1 I love American movies. ☐
  _____
  2 Do you like cook? ☐
  _____
  3 Pedro doesn't like basketball. ☐
  _____
  4 I hate be late. ☐
  _____
  5 Tomiko enjoys to play soccer. ☐
  _____
  6 I love talking to my friends. ☐
  _____

◀ Go back to page 27

GRAMMAR PRACTICE

4A Prepositions of time

We use different prepositions to make common time expressions.

▶ 4.2

Preposition	We use this with ...	Example
in	*the* + parts of the day	in the morning(s) in the afternoon(s) in the evening(s)
	the + seasons	in the winter in the spring in the summer in the fall
	months of the year	in January in September
on	days of the week	on Monday(s) on Tuesday(s)
	days and parts of the day	on Thursday morning(s) on Saturday night(s) on Friday evening(s) on New Year's Day
	the weekend	on the weekend / on weekends
at	times	at 6 o'clock at 11:30
	midnight/noon/night	at midnight at noon / noon at night
	festivals	at Thanksgiving at New Year's
from ... to	days	from Wednesday to Sunday
	months	from January to June
	times	from 6:30 to 9:00
	years	from 2000 to 2006

Look! at night NOT ~~in night~~ BUT on Friday night

We use these time expressions at the start or at the end of a sentence. We use a comma after them if they are at the start.

I usually get up at 7:30.
At 7:30, I usually get up.
I have an Italian class on Wednesday evening.
On Wednesday evening, I have an Italian class.

We can use plurals for days, parts of the day, and *weekend* if we talk about things that we do regularly.

I don't work on the weekend / on weekends.
In the morning / In the mornings, I often go running before work.

118

1 Complete the sentences with *in*, *on*, *at*, or *from ... to*.
   1 I usually take a shower _____ the evening.
   2 Charles does his homework _____ night.
   3 I'm at work _____ 8:30 _____ 6:30 every day.
   4 They visit their cousins _____ New Year's Day.
   5 We always go out _____ Friday nights.
   6 Is it hot here _____ August?
   7 The days are short _____ the winter.
   8 What do you like doing _____ the weekend?

2 Read the text and underline eight mistakes. Write the correct prepositions below the text.

Every day, from Monday in Friday, I get up at 6:30. I leave the house at 7:30, and I start work on 8:15. I don't work on Friday afternoons. I finish work in noon.

On July and August, it's very hot. I usually go to the swimming pool with my children in the afternoons, and in night, we go for a walk.

In the weekend, I don't get up early. At Saturday mornings, I go running on 11, and then my wife and I make lunch. On Sundays, we usually take the children to visit my parents or my wife's parents.

1 _____   4 _____   7 _____
2 _____   5 _____   8 _____
3 _____   6 _____

3 Write sentences. Add prepositions.
   1 I visit my grandparents / the weekend
   _____
   2 February / we usually go skiing
   _____
   3 I usually stop for a cup of coffee / noon
   _____
   4 Wednesday evenings / my sister does yoga
   _____
   5 Carlos works / Monday / Saturday
   _____
   6 My daughter's birthday is / the spring
   _____

◀ Go back to page 31

GRAMMAR PRACTICE

4C Present continuous

We use the present continuous to talk about:
- things that are happening now.

I'm taking a shower.
It's raining.
What are you reading?

- things that are temporary.

We're staying in a hotel.
I'm not working this week.

We form the present continuous with the verb *be* + the *-ing* form of the main verb.

▶ 4.9	I	he / she / it	you / we / they
+	I'm getting dressed.	He's getting dressed.	We're getting dressed.
−	I'm not watching TV.	She's not watching TV.	We're not watching TV.
?	Am I sleeping?	Is she sleeping?	Are they sleeping?
Y/N	Yes, I am. / No, I'm not.	Yes, she is. / No, she's not/isn't.	Yes, they are. / No, they're not/aren't.

Spelling rules for the *-ing* form

We usually add *-ing* to the base form of the verb.

play ⇒ playing   talk ⇒ talking

When a verb ends in consonant + *e*, we usually remove the *e* and then add *-ing*.

take ⇒ taking   live ⇒ living
BUT *be* ⇒ being

When a one-syllable verb ends in a vowel + a consonant, we double the consonant and then add *-ing*.

sit ⇒ sitting   plan ⇒ planning

Look! We often use the present continuous with time expressions such as (*right*) *now*, *today*, *this week/month/year*, and *at the moment*.
I'm having breakfast right now.
I'm studying a lot this month.

1 Put the words in the correct order to make sentences.
  1 using / the computer / Ella / is / ?
  _____
  2 parents / I / visiting / am / my
  _____
  3 reading / Matt / the newspaper / is
  _____
  4 isn't / my / working / phone
  _____
  5 staying / we / are / at a hotel / this weekend
  _____
  6 you / going / where / are / ?
  _____

2 Complete the sentences with the correct present continuous forms of the verbs in parentheses.
  1 I _____ dinner right now. (have)
  2 We _____ to the beach now. (go)
  3 The Internet _____ today. (not work)
  4 _____ Tim _____ a shower? (take)
  5 She _____ a coat today. (not wear)
  6 What _____ you _____? (do)
  7 I _____ today because it's Saturday. (not study)
  8 _____ I _____ in the right place? (sit)

3 Look at the picture. Use the words to make questions and write true short answers.

  1 they / talk
  _____
  2 they / have / a good time
  _____
  3 it / snow
  _____
  4 it / rain
  _____
  5 she / carry / an umbrella
  _____
  6 he / wear / glasses
  _____

◀ Go back to page 35

GRAMMAR PRACTICE

5A Simple present and present continuous

We use the simple present to talk about facts and things that happen regularly.

Sam lives in Australia.
We wear a uniform at work.
I usually wake up at six o'clock.

We use the present continuous to talk about things that are happening now, or are temporary.

I'm wearing blue pants today.
I'm going to work by car today.
My friend is living in New York right now.

We often use the simple present and present continuous together to contrast the usual situation with what is happening now, or is temporary.

▶ 5.2 **Present simple and present continuous**

It **usually doesn't** rain in the summer,	but it**'s raining** today.
I **usually wear** jeans to work,	but today I**'m wearing** a suit.
I **often don't** cook,	but I**'m cooking** every evening this week.

There are some verbs that describe a state, not an action. We normally don't use these verbs in the present continuous.

I prefer this music. NOT ~~I'm preferring this music~~.
Sorry, I don't understand. NOT ~~Sorry, I'm not understanding~~.
I have some new sandals. NOT ~~I'm having some new sandals~~.

> **Look!** Here are some common state verbs:
> **Feelings:** *like, love, hate, want, prefer, need*
> **Thoughts and opinions:** *know, believe, remember, forget, understand, think*
> **States:** *be, belong, have* (when we talk about relationships or possessions)

1 Choose the correct words to complete the sentences and questions.
1. What *do you do* / *are you doing* right now?
2. *Is he going* / *Does he go* there often?
3. They *'re working* / *work* late tonight.
4. I *never read* / *'m never reading* books.
5. I *'m studying* / *study* in my bedroom now.
6. Most people *finish* / *are finishing* school at eighteen or nineteen years old.

2 Complete the sentences with the simple present or present continuous form of the verbs in parentheses.
1. I _____ right now. (read)
2. He _____ to New York three times a year. (go)
3. They _____ us every summer. (visit)
4. How _____ Erica _____ to work today? (get)
5. I _____ coffee very often. (not drink)
6. We _____ a really good TV series right now. (watch)
7. I usually _____ juice for breakfast. (have)
8. Please be quiet – the baby _____. (sleep)

3 Read the information. Then complete the text about James.

James usually [1]_____ tea and toast for breakfast. He [2]_____ a suit. He [3]_____ all day. This week, James is on vacation. He [4]_____ coffee and croissants for breakfast. He [5]_____ shorts and a T-shirt. He [6]_____ a great time!

120

◀ Go back to page 41

5C can and can't

We use *can* and *can't* to talk about:

- ability.

I can swim.
My brother can play the guitar.
I can't speak Italian.
My sister can't cook.

- possibility.

You can make money from your hobby.
It can snow here in the winter.
You can't get there by bus.

- permission.

You can take my umbrella.
We can sit here.
We can't park on this street.
You can't use this gym if you're not a member.

To make questions with *can*, we put *can* before the subject. We use the same form for all people.

▶ 5.8   I / you / he / she / it / we / they

+	I **can play** the piano.
	They **can go** to the city by bus.
	We **can finish** work early today.
−	She **can't speak** Japanese.
	They **can't work** at night.
	You **can't walk** on the grass.
?	**Can** she **play** the guitar?
	Can you **come** to my party?
	Can we **park** the car here?
Y/N	Yes, we **can**. / No, we **can't**.

Look! The full form of *can't* is *cannot*. We don't often use *cannot*; *can't* is the usual negative form.
I can't meet you tonight. NOT ~~I cannot meet you tonight~~.

1 Look at the chart and complete the sentences with *can* or *can't*.

	Craig	Helen	Manuel	Silvia
cook	✔	✔	✘	✔
play tennis	✔	✘	✔	✘
drive	✔	✔	✔	✘
speak French	✘	✘	✘	✔

1 Craig _____ cook, but he _____ speak French.
2 Helen _____ play tennis, but she _____ drive.
3 Craig, Helen, and Manuel _____ speak French.
4 Manuel _____ cook, but he _____ drive.
5 Silvia _____ cook and speak French.
6 Craig, Helen, and Manuel _____ drive.

2 Write short answers to the questions about the people in exercise 1.

1 Can Silvia drive? _____
2 Can Craig play tennis? _____
3 Can Helen cook? _____
4 Can Manuel speak French? _____
5 Can Helen and Silvia play tennis? _____
6 Can Craig and Manuel drive? _____

3 Complete the sentences about the pictures. Use *can* or *can't* and the phrases in the box.

> walk on the grass   ride a bike on this street
> pay with a credit card   park here for one hour

1 You _____
2 You _____
3 You _____
4 You _____

◀ Go back to page 45

GRAMMAR PRACTICE

6A there is/there are, some/any/no, prepositions of place

We use *there is* to say that something singular exists.

There's a sofa in the living room.
There's a small balcony in my apartment.

We use *there are* for the plural form.

There are five people in my family.
There are three bedrooms in her apartment.

We use *some* and *any* with plural nouns. We use *some* in affirmative sentences when more than one thing or person exists, but we don't say exactly how many.

There are some chairs in the classroom.
There are some new students in our class.
I have some books in my bag.

We use *any* in negative sentences and questions with plural nouns. We use *no* after an affirmative verb and with a singular or plural noun.

There are no tables. / There aren't any tables.
I have no brothers or sisters. / I don't have any brothers or sisters.
Are there any shelves in the bedroom?

▶ 6.3

	Singular nouns	Plural nouns
+	**There's** a shelf in my bedroom.	**There are some** shelves in the kitchen.
−	**There's no** chair in my bedroom.	**There are no / There aren't any** chairs in the kitchen.
?	**Is there** a cabinet in your bedroom?	**Are there any** cabinets in the kitchen?
Y/N	Yes, **there is**. / No, **there's not/ there isn't**.	Yes, **there are**. / No, **there aren't**.

Prepositions of place

▶ 6.7 We use prepositions of place to describe location.

The window is across from the door.

in front of   under   next to   in

on   between   behind   across from

1 Read the advertisement and then complete the sentences with *there's a/there are* and *there's/there are no*.

> Third-floor two-bedroom apartment in a popular area near stores and a park. Five-minute walk to subway station. Living room with big windows. Kitchen, bathroom (shower only, no bathtub). Empty – ready to move in!

1 _____ two bedrooms.
2 _____ bathroom.
3 _____ a backyard, but _____ park near the apartment.
4 _____ some big windows in the living room.
5 _____ bathtub in the bathroom.
6 _____ people in the apartment right now.
7 _____ some stores near the apartment.
8 _____ subway station near the apartment.

2 Complete the questions and answers about an apartment.

1 _____ garage in your apartment building?
No, _____.
2 _____ shelves in the living room?
Yes, _____.
3 _____ basement that you can use?
Yes, _____.
4 _____ sofa in the living room?
Yes, _____.
5 _____ good restaurants in the area?
No, _____.
6 _____ schools for the children?
Yes, _____.

3 Look at the floor plan of a house. Complete the sentences with prepositions of place.

front yard	living room	kitchen	dining room	
				backyard
front yard	bedroom	bathroom	bedroom	

1 The kitchen is _____ the bathroom.
2 The bathroom is _____ the two bedrooms.
3 The dining room is _____ the kitchen.
4 There is a small yard _____ the house.
5 There is a large yard _____ the house.
6 There are some trees _____ the large yard.

◀ Go back to page 49

6C Modifiers

We use modifiers with adjectives to make them stronger or weaker.

It's really/very big.

It's pretty big.

It's not very big.

It's not big at all.

We use *really* and *very* to make an adjective stronger.
The city is really big.
The market is very busy on Saturdays.

We use *pretty* and *not very* to make an adjective weaker. If we use *pretty*, the adjective has the same meaning, but is weaker. If we use *not very*, the adjective has the opposite meaning.

The bridge is pretty old.
The apartment's not very old. = The apartment is pretty new.

We use *not* + adjective + *at all* to give a strong opposite meaning to an adjective.
The beach isn't crowded at all. = The beach is very empty.
The restaurant's not expensive at all. = The restaurant is very cheap.

▶ 6.12

modifier + adjective	modifier + adjective + (singular) noun
The house is **really**/**very beautiful**.	It's a **really**/**very beautiful** house.
The house is **pretty beautiful**.	It's a **pretty beautiful** house.
The house is**n't very beautiful**.	It**'s not** a **very beautiful** house.
The house is**n't beautiful at all**.	It**'s not** a **beautiful** house **at all**.

GRAMMAR PRACTICE

1 Rewrite the sentences. Put the modifier in parentheses in the correct place.
1 The beach is busy today. (very)
2 The stadium is full at the moment. (not very)
3 You can buy beautiful presents at the market. (really)
4 This is an old apartment building. (pretty)
5 This café is expensive. (not … at all)
6 I'm reading an interesting book right now. (pretty)

2 Put the words in the correct order to make sentences.
1 a / bathroom / there / large / is / pretty
2 a / skyscraper / I / in / very / tall / work
3 I / street / on / a / live / quiet / pretty
4 clothes / are / these / very / expensive
5 sister / at / isn't / my / busy / all
6 food / good / the / isn't / very

3 Look at Andy's review of his vacation. Complete the sentences about it using modifiers and the adjectives in parentheses.

The old town is ¹_____*really beautiful*_____ (beautiful), but it's ²_____ (busy). The restaurants are ³_____ (expensive), and the food is ⁴_____ (good). The beaches are ⁵_____ (crowded), but they're ⁶_____ (clean). It's ⁷_____ (good) place for families because it's ⁸_____ (cheap) place to stay.

◀ Go back to page 53

VOCABULARY PRACTICE

1A Countries and nationalities

1 ▶ 1.2 Complete the chart with the nationalities in the box. Listen and check.

> Portuguese British Mexican French Argentinian
> Polish Chinese Italian Brazilian Spanish

Country	Nationality
1 China	_____
2 Japan	Japanese
3 Portugal	_____
4 Vietnam	Vietnamese
5 England	English
6 Ireland	Irish
7 Poland	_____
8 Scotland	Scottish
9 Spain	_____
10 Turkey	Turkish
11 the UK	_____
12 Germany	German
13 Mexico	_____
14 the U.S.	American
15 Argentina	_____
16 Australia	Australian
17 Brazil	_____
18 Canada	Canadian
19 Colombia	Colombian
20 Egypt	Egyptian
21 Peru	Peruvian
22 Italy	_____
23 Russia	Russian
24 France	_____

2 Complete the sentences about the people.

1 Diego is Peruvian. He's from _____.
2 Natasha is Russian. She's from _____.
3 Troy is American. He's from _____.
4 Mesut is Turkish. He's from _____.
5 Dominique and Ellie are Canadian. They're from _____.
6 Ana is Colombian. She's from _____.
7 Maciek and Janusz are Polish. They're from _____.
8 Hong is Vietnamese. She's from _____.
9 Oscar and Ana are Brazilian. They're from _____.
10 José Carlos is Mexican. He's from _____.

◀ Go back to page 4

1A Numbers 1–1,000

1 ▶ 1.7 Write the missing numbers. Listen and check.

0	zero/oh	21	twenty-one
1	one	22	twenty-two
2	two	23	_____
3	three	30	thirty
4	four	31	_____
5	five	32	thirty-two
6	six	40	forty
7	seven	50	_____
8	eight	60	sixty
9	nine	70	seventy
10	ten	80	eighty
11	_____	90	ninety
12	twelve	100	a hundred/one hundred
13	thirteen	101	a hundred and one
14	fourteen	102	_____
15	_____	200	two hundred
16	sixteen	210	two hundred and ten
17	seventeen	322	_____
18	eighteen	468	four hundred and sixty-eight
19	nineteen	713	_____
20	_____	1,000	a thousand/one thousand

We often pronounce zero "oh" when we say numbers one at a time: "I'm in room four-oh-three." (=403)

2 Look at the pictures and complete the numbers in words.

1 It's Lucy's birthday. She's _____.

5 A normal year has _____ days.

2 The Jones family live on _____, Main Street.

6 It's _____ kilometers to Paris.

3 The population of Newtown is _____.

7 Our hotel room is number _____.

4 The bike is _____ dollars.

8 The watch is _____ euros.

◀ Go back to page 5

VOCABULARY PRACTICE

1C Personal objects

1 ▶1.9 Match the words in the box with pictures 1–20. Listen and check.

| key | sunglasses | mirror | gloves | chewing gum | flashlight | tissues | photo | stamps | glasses |
| identity card | watch | umbrella | hairbrush | wallet | candy | change purse | comb | tablet | cell phone |

1 _____ 2 _____ 3 _____ 4 _____ 5 _____

6 _____ 7 _____ 8 _____ 9 _____ 10 _____

11 _____ 12 _____ 13 _____ 14 _____ 15 _____

16 _____ 17 _____ 18 _____ 19 _____ 20 _____

2 Read the information about plurals. Write plurals for the words.

Look! We make most plurals by adding -s or -es. We add -es if a word ends in -ch, -sh, -s, -x, or -z:
stamp ⇨ stamps, watch ⇨ watches.

1 comb _____
2 hairbrush _____
3 card _____
4 key _____
5 mirror _____
6 cell phone _____
7 photo _____
8 change purse _____
9 tablet _____
10 flashlight _____
11 umbrella _____
12 wallet _____

4 ▶1.10 Now read about the pronunciation of plurals ending in -s and -es. Put the plurals from exercise 2 into the chart. Listen and check.

/s/	/z/	/ɪz/
when the final sound in the word is /t/, /k/, /p/, /f/, or /θ/	when the final sound in the word is /b/, /d/, /g/, /l/, /m/, /n/, /v/, /ð/, or a vowel sound	when the final sound in the word is /tʃ/, /dʒ/, /ʒ/, /ʃ/, /s/, /ks/, or /z/
	combs	

3 Choose the correct words to complete the sentences.
1 Is that rain? Where's my *umbrella* / *hairbrush*?
2 Look at this *photo* / *mirror* of my boyfriend.
3 Do you have a *tablet* / *stamp*? I want to send a letter.
4 What time is it? I don't have my *wallet* / *watch*.
5 It's very cold today. Take some *mirrors* / *gloves* with you.
6 I always wear *combs* / *glasses* when I read.
7 Where's my car *key* / *card*?
8 I have twenty dollars in my *change purse* / *flashlight*.
9 It's very sunny. Where are my *tablets* / *sunglasses*?
10 *Chewing gum* / *Candy* is bad for your teeth.

◀ Go back to page 8

137

VOCABULARY PRACTICE

2A Jobs and job verbs

1 ▶ 2.1 Match the jobs in the box with pictures 1–20. Listen and check.

> hairdresser   tour guide   police officer   doctor   electrician   teacher   taxi driver   dentist   flight attendant   singer   mechanic
> nurse   lawyer   waiter/waitress   receptionist   businessperson   accountant   construction worker   chef   salesclerk

1 _____

2 _____

3 _____

4 _____

5 _____

6 _____

7 _____

8 _____

9 _____

10 _____

11 _____

12 _____

13 _____

14 _____

15 _____

16 _____

17 _____

18 _____

19 _____

20 _____

2 ▶ 2.2 Match the two parts to make sentences. Listen and check.

1 He cooks
2 He drives
3 He fixes
4 They make
5 She serves
6 He wears
7 They start
8 She teaches
9 He finishes
10 He cuts
11 She helps
12 She sells

a a taxi.
b food in a restaurant.
c English in a school.
d work at 9 a.m.
e people's hair.
f food to customers.
g people at a tourist office.
h cars in a garage.
i computers in a store.
j a suit at work.
k clothes in a factory.
l work at 6 p.m.

3 Complete the sentences with job verbs and jobs.

1 Mario works in a garage. He _____ cars. He's a _____.
2 Samantha works in a high school. She _____ French and Spanish. She's a _____.
3 Hitoshi and Kazuo work in the kitchen of a restaurant. They _____ the food for the customers. They are _____.
4 Tomiko also works in the restaurant. She _____ the customers in the restaurant. She's a _____.
5 Maya is a _____. She _____ people's hair.
6 Terry works at night. He _____ a taxi in different places in New York. He's a _____.
7 Raul works in a clothing store. He _____ clothes. He's a _____.
8 Ola, Piotr, and Marta are in a pop group. Marta plays the drums, Piotr plays the guitar, and Ola _____. She's the group's _____.
9 Mark works on airplanes. He _____ a uniform. He _____ food and drink to the passengers. He's a _____.
10 Clara works in a hospital. She _____ work at 7 p.m., and she _____ late, at 8:30 p.m. She's not a doctor. She's a _____.

◀ Go back to page 13

VOCABULARY PRACTICE

2B Activities (1)

1 ▶ 2.7 Look at pictures 1–20 and complete the phrases with the words in the box. Listen and check.

> study   book   (my) friends   read   time   walk   guitar   movie   TV
> dinner   watch   play   radio   listen   running   coffee   movie   relax

1 go to the _____   2 go out for _____   3 go out for _____   4 go out for a _____   5 go _____   6 _____ to music

7 listen to the _____   8 spend _____ with my family   9 _____ tennis   10 play the _____   11 _____ the newspaper   12 read a _____

13 _____   14 see a _____   15 _____   16 meet _____   17 _____ soccer   18 watch _____

2 Complete the sentences with phrases from exercise 1. Use the correct form.
1 My sister _____ in a band. She's really good.
2 My dad always _____ at breakfast. He likes reading the sports section.
3 We _____ on Saturday evenings. We go to a very good Chinese restaurant.
4 I want to get some exercise. Do you want to _____ with me in the park?
5 I _____ all the time. I'm a Barcelona fan.
6 I _____ in the car. I play my favorite songs.
7 After work on Fridays, I _____ in town, and we go to a café to talk.
8 On the weekend, Rosie _____: her parents, her brother, and her two sisters.
9 My sister and I _____ on Saturdays. I usually have a cappuccino, and she has a latte.
10 I _____ in the library after class.

3 Correct the mistakes in the sentences. Rewrite the sentences.
1 My friend Tara plays a guitar in a rock group.
_____
2 Do you want to watch movie tonight?
_____
3 I always listen music on the train.
_____
4 I usually meet the friends after work.
_____
5 I want to go the movies this weekend.
_____
6 My parents play the tennis with their friends.
_____

◀ Go back to page 14

VOCABULARY PRACTICE

3A Family

1 ▶ 3.2 Complete Jack's family tree with the words in the box. Listen and check.

| wife   father-in-law   sister-in-law   daughter   brother   sister   nephew   niece   father   aunt   cousin (×2)   grandmother |

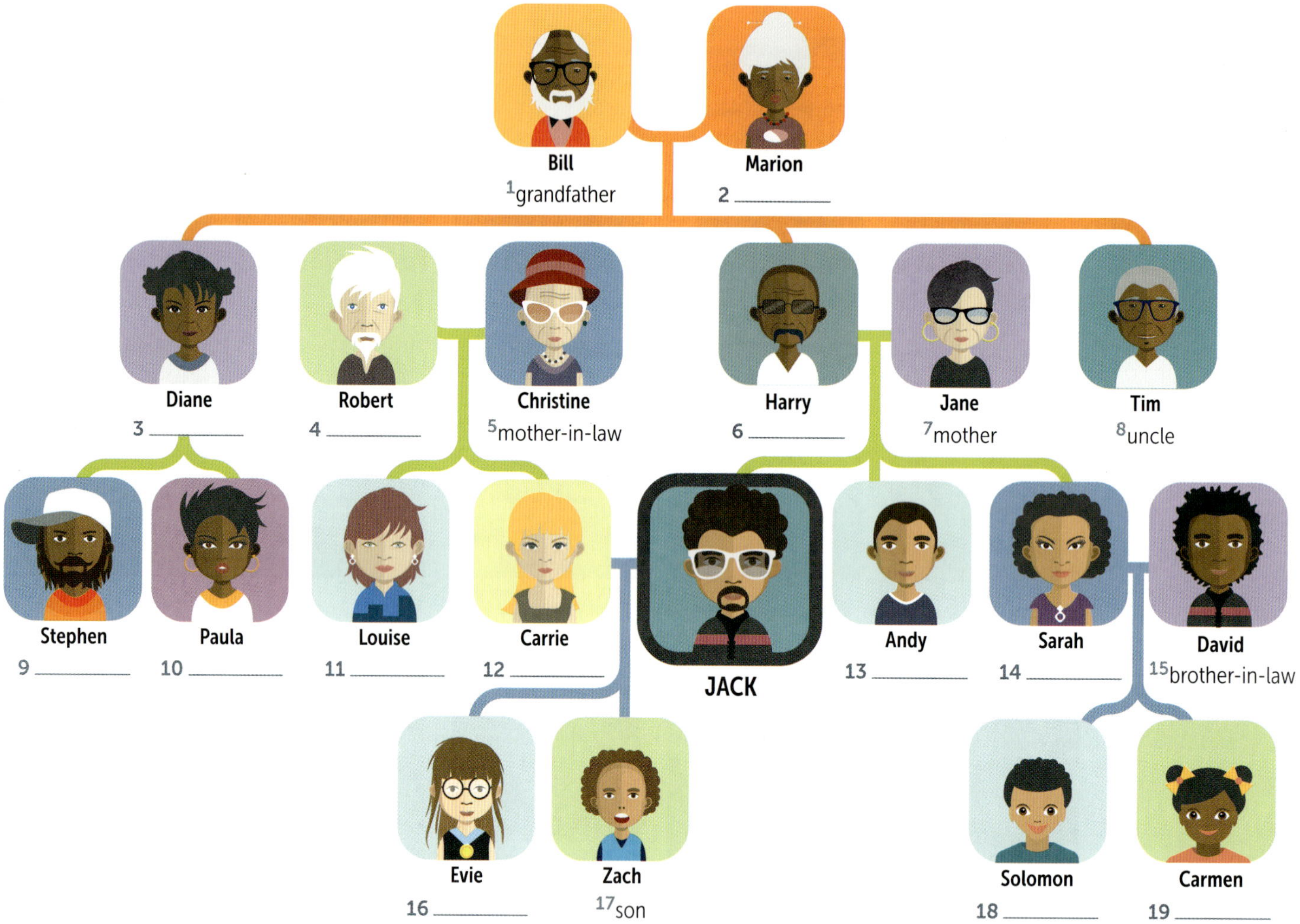

Bill — [1]grandfather
Marion — 2 _____

Diane — 3 _____
Robert — 4 _____
Christine — [5]mother-in-law
Harry — 6 _____
Jane — [7]mother
Tim — [8]uncle

Stephen — 9 _____
Paula — 10 _____
Louise — 11 _____
Carrie — 12 _____
JACK
Andy — 13 _____
Sarah — 14 _____
David — [15]brother-in-law

Evie — 16 _____
Zach — [17]son
Solomon — 18 _____
Carmen — 19 _____

2 ▶ 3.3 Complete the sentences with the correct names.

1 _____ and _____ are Jack's parents.
2 _____ and _____ are Jack's in-laws (mother- and father-in-law).
3 _____ and _____ are Jack's grandparents.
4 _____ and _____ are Jack's children.
5 _____, _____, _____ and _____ are Harry and Jane's grandchildren.
6 Jack is _____ and _____'s son-in-law.
7 Carrie is _____ and _____'s daughter-in-law.
8 Jack is _____'s husband.
9 _____, _____ and _____ are Bill and Marion's grandsons.
10 _____ is Robert and Christine's granddaughter.

3 Complete the chart with the family words from exercises 1 and 2.

male	female	male and female

4 Find three false definitions. Write the correct definitions.

1 My nephew is my brother's son. _____
2 My mother-in-law is my wife's sister. _____
3 My daughter is my son's sister. _____
4 My granddaughter is my daughter's daughter. _____
5 My niece is my cousin's daughter. _____
6 My father-in-law is my husband's father. _____
7 My grandparents are my nephew's parents. _____
8 My cousins are my aunt's children. _____

◀ Go back to page 23

140

VOCABULARY PRACTICE

3C Activities (2)

1 ▶ 3.7 Match the phrases below with pictures a–p. Listen and check.

do	play	go	have	visit
1 karate _____	4 golf _____	7 bowling _____	12 a barbecue _____	14 a gallery _____
2 yoga _____	5 volleyball _____	8 bike riding _____	13 a picnic _____	15 a museum _____
walk	6 the violin _____	9 dancing _____		16 relatives _____
3 the dog _____		10 shopping _____		
		11 swimming _____		

2 Complete the sentences with the verbs in the correct form.
 1 They _____ a barbecue every time it's hot and sunny.
 2 We always _____ a picnic for my birthday.
 3 I _____ yoga on Friday mornings.
 4 We _____ volleyball on the beach.
 5 I sometimes _____ galleries.
 6 I always _____ dancing with my family on Saturday evenings.
 7 My son _____ the violin in his school orchestra.
 8 I don't go to the gym, but I _____ dancing on weekends.
 9 My best friend _____ bike riding every Sunday afternoon.
 10 My children often _____ bowling with their friends.

3 Write the phrases from exercise 1 that match the sentences.
 1 If you're interested in very old things, you can do this.
 _____
 2 This is when you go to see your cousins, grandparents, etc.
 _____
 3 Lots of people do this Japanese sport.
 _____
 4 Lots of people do this sport on the beach in the summer.
 _____
 5 You can do this in the sea or at a pool.
 _____
 6 This is when you cook a meal outside.
 _____
 7 You need a bicycle for this.
 _____
 8 You need a very large open green space if you want to do this sport.
 _____

◀ Go back to page 26

VOCABULARY PRACTICE

4A Daily routine verbs

1 ▶ 4.1 Match pictures a–o with activities 1–15. Listen and check.

1 have lunch ____
2 have dinner ____
3 go to school ____
4 get dressed ____
5 wake up ____
6 take a shower ____
7 get up ____
8 go to work ____
9 take a bath ____
10 go to bed ____
11 go to sleep ____
12 finish school ____
13 get home ____
14 finish work ____
15 have breakfast ____

◀ Go back to page 30

4B The weather and the seasons

1 ▶ 4.5 Look at the pictures and complete the sentences with the cities. Listen and check.

22° BARCELONA | -11° ST PETERSBURG | 14° SHANGHAI | 36° MUMBAI | 12° SAN FRANCISCO | 10° LIVERPOOL | 1° STOCKHOLM

1 It's raining/rainy in _____.
2 It's snowing/snowy in _____.
3 It's hot in _____.
4 It's warm in _____.
5 It's very cold in _____.
6 It's wet in _____.
7 It's sunny in _____.
8 It's foggy in _____.
9 It's windy in _____.
10 It's cloudy in _____.
11 It's icy in _____.
12 It's cold in _____.

2 Label the pictures with the seasons. Then write a word from exercise 1 to describe the weather in each season.

summer   fall   spring   winter

_____, _____   _____, _____   _____, _____   _____, _____

◀ Go back to page 32

VOCABULARY PRACTICE

5A Clothes

1 ▶ 5.1 Label the clothes and jewelry in the pictures with the words in the box. Listen and check.

> belt   tie   necklace   bracelet   pants   T-shirt   earrings   boots   coat   jacket   jeans   sandals   blouse
> sneakers   scarf   jewelry   dress   gloves   hat   shirt   shoes   shorts   skirt   socks   suit   sweater

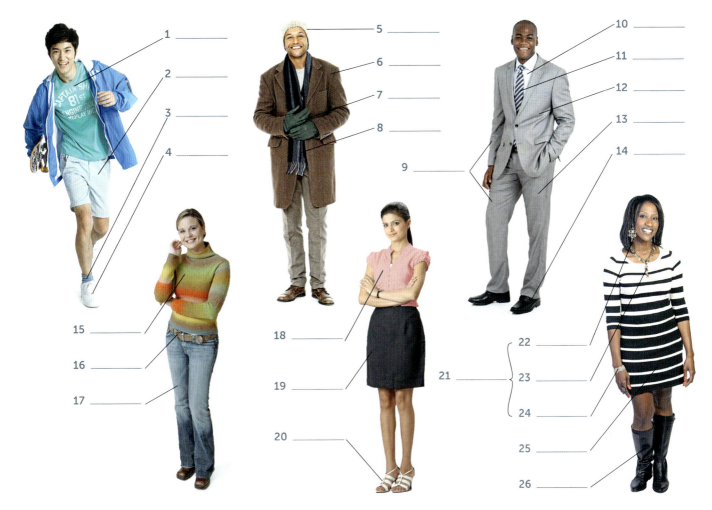

2 Choose the correct words to complete the sentences.

1 My pants are too big. I need a *necklace / belt*.
2 Jim hates wearing a suit and *tie / scarf*. He prefers jeans and a T-shirt.
3 When Anna goes running, she wears *boots / sneakers*.
4 I like wearing jewelry, especially *sandals / earrings*.
5 It's cold outside. Wear a scarf and *gloves / shorts*.
6 My daughter likes climbing trees, so she wears *pants / a skirt*.
7 Sally's going to a party, so she's wearing a *T-shirt / dress*.
8 In the summer, I like wearing *shorts / shoes* and sandals.
9 Should I wear my red *blouse / socks* or my blue shirt with my jeans?
10 You need to wear a *coat / suit* when you go to a job interview.

◀ Go back to page 40

5A Ordinal numbers

1 ▶ 5.4 Write the ordinal numbers. Listen and check.

1 first
2 _____
3 third
4 _____
5 _____
6 sixth
7 seventh

8 _____
9 _____
10 tenth
11 _____
12 _____
13 thirteenth
14 fourteenth

15 _____
20 twentieth
21 _____
22 twenty-second
30 thirtieth
40 _____
50 fiftieth

2 Complete the sentences with the ordinal numbers in parentheses. Write them in words.

1 Kazakhstan is the _____ biggest country in the world. (9)
2 December is the _____ month of the year. (12)
3 Barack Obama was the _____ president of the U.S. (44)
4 International Women's Day is March _____. (8)
5 Valentine's Day is on February _____. (14)
6 Veterans Day is November _____. (11)

◀ Go back to page 41

143

VOCABULARY PRACTICE

5C Hobbies

1 ▶ 5.7 Match the verbs in the box with pictures 1–15. You need some verbs more than once. Listen and check.

collect play make sew knit sing dance take write paint draw bake

1 _____

2 _____

3 _____ online games

4 _____

5 _____ photos

6 _____ a blog

7 _____ the drums

8 _____ jewelry

9 _____

10 _____ chess

11 _____

12 _____

13 _____ stamps

14 _____

15 _____ coins

2 Match the hobbies with the descriptions.

1 These hobbies are connected to music.
　_____
2 People often do these hobbies in beautiful places.
　_____
3 This hobby is connected to food.
　_____
4 You study and collect objects for this hobby.
　_____
5 You need another person to do this hobby.
　_____
6 These hobbies are connected to clothes.
　_____
7 You need to use the Internet for this hobby.
　_____

3 Choose the correct words to complete the sentences.

1 Right now, I'm *drawing* / *knitting* a sweater. I want to finish it before the winter.
2 I collect *stamps* / *coins*. My favorite one is made of gold.
3 Everyone can *sew* / *take photos* on their smartphones, but some people can do it really well.
4 My friend Emily *makes* / *sews* jewelry. She's making me a necklace for my birthday.
5 We need someone who *plays the drums* / *bakes* for our band. Do you know anyone?
6 My cousin is traveling in Africa at the moment, and she *makes* / *writes* a blog every day. I like reading it to find out what she's doing.
7 My wife loves *painting* / *baking,* and I love eating her cakes and cookies. We're a perfect match!
8 My friend Matt is learning to *dance* / *sing*. Right now, he's learning the tango.

144
◀ Go back to page 44

VOCABULARY PRACTICE

6A Rooms and furniture

1 ▶ 6.1 Label the picture with the rooms and places in the box. Listen and check.

| front yard | balcony | kitchen | bedroom | living room | bathroom (x2) | dining room | study | garage | hall | attic | basement | stairs |

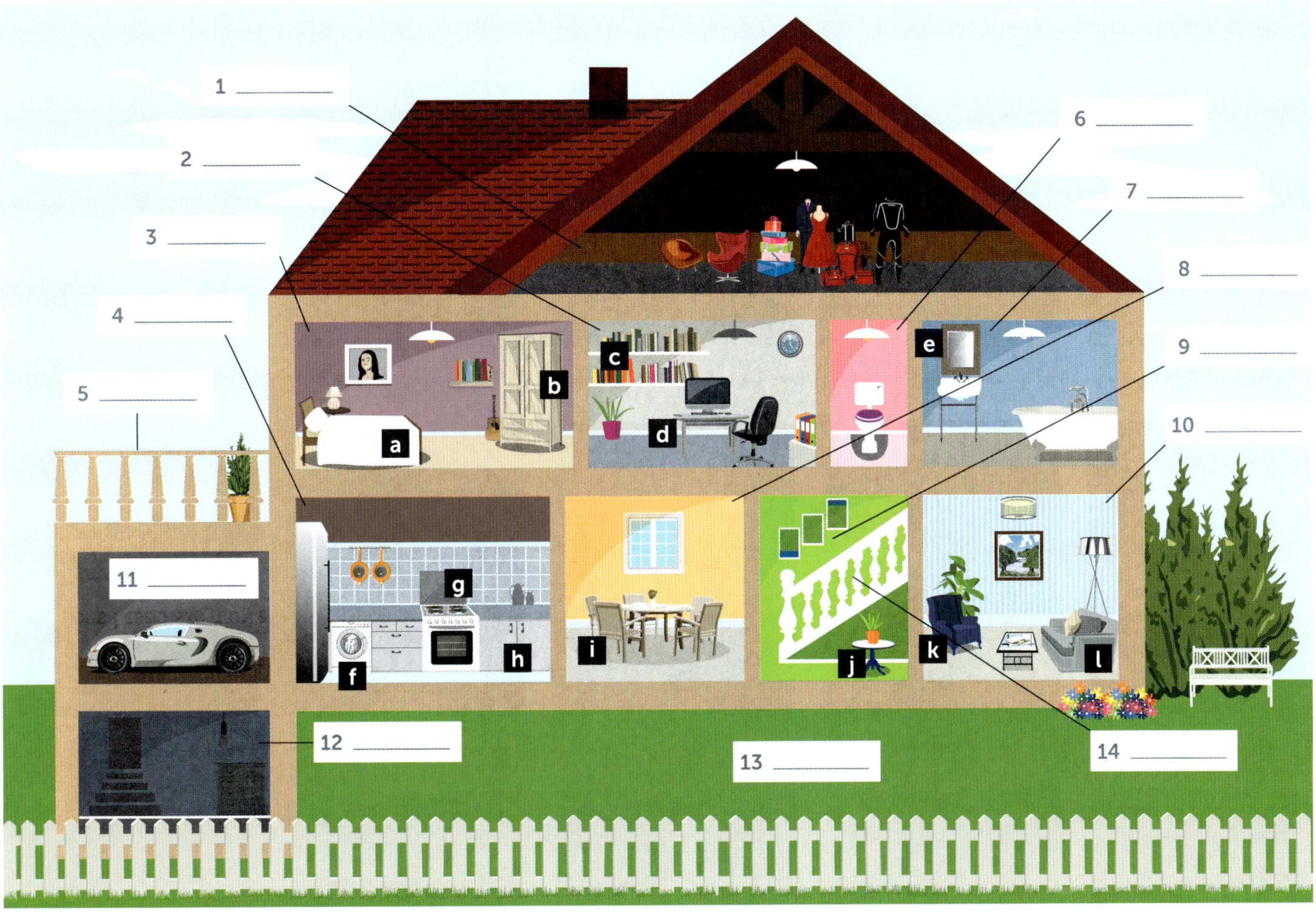

2 ▶ 6.2 Find the furniture items in the picture. Write the letters a–l. Listen and check.

1 armchair _____
2 bed _____
3 chairs _____
4 stove _____
5 cabinets _____
6 desk _____
7 shelves _____
8 sofa _____
9 table _____
10 closet _____
11 washing machine _____
12 mirror _____

◀ Go back to page 48

6B Common adjectives

1 ▶ 6.8 Match the adjectives with their opposites. Listen and check.

1 expensive
2 clean
3 narrow
4 noisy
5 comfortable
6 heavy
7 modern

a wide
b uncomfortable
c light
d cheap
e traditional
f dirty
g quiet

2 Complete the sentences with opposite adjectives.

1 I don't like _____ restaurants. I like _____ places where you can talk with friends.
2 My girlfriend usually buys _____ clothes. I'm different – I buy _____ clothes and have some money for other things.
3 We have two sofas. One is old, but very _____ – it's perfect for watching a movie. The other one is new, but it's _____.
4 My husband wants to buy some _____ furniture, but I don't. I want some _____ things because our apartment is very new.
5 Your T-shirt is really _____! Go and find a _____ blouse.
6 My bike is very _____, but Carl's is really _____. I can carry his bike with one hand.
7 I only have a double bed and a small closet in my bedroom. The room's _____ and the bed's _____, so I have no space.

◀ Go back to page 50

145

VOCABULARY PRACTICE

6C Places in a city

1 ▶ 6.15 Match the places in the box with pictures 1–14. Listen and check.

> apartment building   bridge   cathedral   concert hall   library   market   monument
> mosque   office building   skyscraper   square   stadium   theater   park

1 _____

2 _____

3 _____

4 _____

5 _____

6 _____

7 _____

8 _____

9 _____

10 _____

11 _____

12 _____

13 _____

14 _____

2 Match the places in a city with the definitions. Some places go with more than one definition.

1. People live here. _____
2. You go here for entertainment. _____, _____, _____
3. This is a religious building. _____, _____
4. This is usually a tall building. _____, _____, _____
5. This can be outdoors or indoors. _____
6. It is very quiet in this building. _____
7. You often find this in the center of a square. _____
8. You can sometimes find restaurants here. _____

3 Complete the sentences with places in a city.

1. This famous _____ is for Abraham Lincoln.
2. Let's go to the _____ and buy some food for a picnic.
3. We live on the ninth floor of this _____.
4. You can see the _____ from about 20 km. away. It's very tall.
5. I work in a small _____ downtown. It has four floors.
6. At the _____, you leave your shoes at the door before you go in.
7. There are concerts and soccer games at this _____.
8. You can walk or ride a bike over this _____, but you can't drive over it.
9. There are concerts in our city's _____ every winter.
10. The central _____ in Wroclaw is really beautiful. There are colorful houses on all four sides.
11. I often go to the _____ to study.

◀ Go back to page 53

COMMUNICATION PRACTICE

1A Student A

1 You are Max. Listen and answer Student B's questions.

Name: Max Lundberg
Nationality: Canadian
Age: 41

2 This is Student B. Ask questions and complete the information.

What's your name? How do you spell it?
_____

Where are you from? _____

How old are you? _____

1C Student A

Look at the people and the possessions. Take turns asking and answering questions with Student B.
Find out who the following possessions belong to. You can only answer *Yes* or *No*.

Is it Eliza's pen?   Are they the children's candies?

Sarah

the students

the children

Eliza

the Johnsons

Tom

Sadiq

the teacher

1D Student A

1 Look at the contacts. Ask Student B for the missing phone numbers and e-mail addresses. Ask for clarification if you don't understand.

A *What's Emi's cell-phone number?*

2 Now listen and answer Student B's questions about the contacts.

Contact	Emi
Mobile	
Email	eesponisa_92@pbmail.com
Contact	Jeff
Mobile	1-917-555-6321
Email	
Contact	Liz
Mobile	
Email	liz.sharp87@pbmail.com
Contact	Ravi
Mobile	1-302-555-8930
Email	

COMMUNICATION PRACTICE

2A Student A

1. Listen to Student B and complete the descriptions.

   Mark is a ¹_____. He ²_____ in a ³_____. He's from ⁴_____, but he ⁵_____ in Toronto. He ⁶_____ in the evening, and he ⁷_____ on the weekend.

   Paula is a ⁸_____. She ⁹_____. She's from ¹⁰_____, but she ¹¹_____ in Manchester. She ¹²_____ in the evening, but she ¹³_____ on the weekend.

2. Now describe these people to your partner.

MAYER
Job: mechanic / fixes cars
Place of work: garage
From: Warsaw
Lives: Berlin
Works: evening ✗ weekend ✓

VIVIANA
Job: teacher / teaches English
Place of work: elementary school
From: Lisbon
Lives: Rio de Janeiro
Works: evening ✗ weekend ✗

2C Student A

1. You want a roommate who has a job, likes music, and cooks. Student B's friend, Jon, needs a room. Ask Student B questions. Is Jon a good roommate for you?

   1. where / he / live?
   2. what / he / do?
   3. what / he / do / free time?
   4. he / cook?
   5. he / like / music?

   bad   OK   good

2. Student B wants a roommate. Your friend, Helen, needs a room. Answer Student B's questions about Helen.

   Helen lives with her mother. She works in an office. After work, she goes to the gym. She doesn't stay at home every night – she goes out a lot with her friends. She doesn't like cats.

3A Student A

1. How often does Flora do these things? Ask Student B.

   A *How often does Flora go to the movies?*
   B *She goes to the movies three times a month.*

2. Answer Student B's questions about Justin.

		Flora	Justin
1	go to the movies		never
2	cook in the evening		four times a week
3	play online games		every day
4	see his/her grandparents		often
5	go running		twice a week
6	listen to the radio		sometimes

3C Student A

Sophia and Sam are a couple. Ask Student B questions about Sam, and answer Student B's questions about Sophia. Find the following:

One thing that Sophia and Sam both love _____
One thing that Sophia and Sam both like _____
One thing that Sophia and Sam both hate _____

A *Does Sam like art?*   B *No. He hates it!*

Sophia

love 😊😊	like 😊	hate ☹☹
art	cook	jazz
walk the dog	soccer	go shopping
have a picnic	go out for dinner	watch TV
do yoga	read magazines	visit family

3D Student A

You want to meet Student B for coffee this weekend. You're free at the following times. Ask and answer questions to find a time when you're both free.

A *Would you like to go out for coffee at 10 o'clock on Saturday morning?*
B *I'm sorry, I can't.*

SATURDAY
Free time
10:00 a.m. – 11:30 a.m.
2:30 p.m. – 3:00 p.m.
6:30 p.m. – 8:30 p.m.
10:00 p.m. – 11:00 p.m.

SUNDAY
Free time
11:00 a.m. – 3:00 p.m.
4:45 p.m. – 6:00 p.m.

COMMUNICATION PRACTICE

4A Student A

1 Look at the pictures of Zak. Ask Student B questions about the missing information. Write the missing times or time expressions. Answer Student B's questions.

A *When does Zak wake up?*
B *He wakes up at ...*

1 _____

2 8:15

3 _____

4 noon

5 _____

6 midnight

7 _____

8 Friday nights

9 _____

10 weekend

11 _____

12 winter

2 Compare with Student B. Do you have the same times?

4C Student A

Take turns describing your picture to Student B and listen to Student B's description. Find six differences between your picture and Student B's picture. Say what the people are doing.

A *In my picture, Clare and John are eating.*
B *In my picture, they're not eating. They're ...*

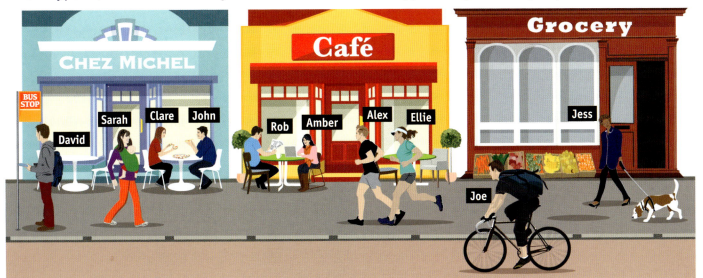

160

COMMUNICATION PRACTICE

5A Student A

1 Look at the pictures. Describe Eric to Student B. Use the words in the boxes to help you.

| have   wear   go to work | | by bike   toast   by bus   jeans and a shirt   a suit   eggs |

Eric usually …   But today, he …

2 Listen to Student B's description. Complete the sentences about Emily.
   1 Emily usually has _____ for breakfast, but today she's having _____.
   2 She usually wears _____, but today she's wearing _____.
   3 She usually goes to work _____, but today she's going _____.

3 Check your pictures and sentences with Student B. Do the sentences describe the pictures correctly?

5C Student A

Ask Student B about Alisha and complete the chart. Answer Student B's questions about Artur.

A *Can Alisha speak a foreign language?*
B *Yes, she can. She can speak Italian.*

Can he/she …	Artur	Alisha
… speak a foreign language?	Yes (English and German)	
… dance?	No	
… play a musical instrument?	No	
… ride a horse?	No	
… take good photos?	Yes	
… cook?	Yes (Polish food)	
… fix things?	Yes (bikes)	

5D Student A

1 You are a customer in a department store. Student B is a salesclerk. Student B begins the conversation. Ask him/her these questions.

- Yes, please. Do you sell coats?
- How much is it?
- Do you have this coat in gray?
- Can I try it on?
- Can I pay with this credit card?
- Great. Thanks.

2 You are a salesclerk in a department store. Student B is a customer. Begin the conversation with him/her. Use these sentences.

- Do you need any help?
- Yes, we do. Here are some in a 28.
- We have them in black, blue, green, and gray.
- Yes, of course.
- They're near the shoes. I'll show you.
- I'm not sure. Let me ask someone. One moment. … They're 60 dollars.

COMMUNICATION PRACTICE

6A Student A

1 Look at the picture and the objects in the box. Ask Student B questions to find out where they are.

| mirror   pictures   books   ball |

A *Is there a mirror above the bed?*   B *No, there's not.*

2 Answer Student B's questions about his/her missing objects. You can only answer *yes* or *no*.

6C Student A

1 A Look at the information about three cities. Ask Student B for the missing information and write it in the chart.

A *Is the market in Blue City busy?*   B *Yes. It's very busy.*

B Answer Student B's questions.

Blue City	Yellowtown	Greenville
mosque – really beautiful ✔	beach – clean?	Old Town – really pretty ✔
market – busy?	restaurants – not very expensive ✘	cathedral – beautiful?
museum – really interesting ✔	local people – friendly?	Central Park – not very clean ✘
art gallery – good?	hotels – really nice ✔	river – clean?
food and drink – not expensive at all ✘	museum – interesting?	monuments – not very famous ✘

2 Decide which city you want to visit in pairs.

A *I want to go to Yellowtown because it has really nice hotels.*   B *Yes, but the beach isn't very clean.*

162

COMMUNICATION PRACTICE

1A Student B

1 This is Student A. Ask questions and complete the information.

What's your name? How do you spell it?
_____

Where are you from? _____

How old are you? _____

2 You are Li. Listen and answer Student A's questions.

Name: Li Yang
Nationality: Chinese
Age: 24

1C Student B

Look at the people and the possessions. Take turns asking and answering questions with Student A.
Find out who the following possessions belong to. You can only answer *Yes* or *No*.

Is it Tom's phone?   Is it the Johnsons' umbrella?

 Sarah
 the students
 the children
 the Johnsons
 Tom
 Sadiq / Eliza / the teacher

1D Student B

1 Look at the contacts. Listen and answer Student A's questions.

2 Now ask Student A for the missing phone numbers and e-mail addresses. Ask for clarification if you don't understand.

B *What's Emi's e-mail address?*

Contact	Emi
Mobile	0034666063267
Email	

Contact	Jeff
Mobile	
Email	jeffreyjones@pbmail.com

Contact	Liz
Mobile	1-310-555-8274
Email	

Contact	Ravi
Mobile	
Email	r.d.g.freelance@pbmail.com

COMMUNICATION PRACTICE

2A Student B

1 Describe these people to your partner.

MARK
Job: nurse / in a hospital
From: Chicago
Lives: Toronto
Works: evening ✓ weekend ✓

PAULA
Job: chef / cooks Japanese food
From: Sydney
Lives: Manchester
Works: evening ✗ weekend ✓

2 Now listen to Student A and complete the descriptions.

Mayer is a [1]_____. He [2]_____ in a [3]_____. He's from [4]_____, but he [5]_____ in Berlin. He [6]_____ in the evening, but he [7]_____ on the weekend.

Viviana is a [8]_____. She [9]_____ in a [10]_____. She's from [11]_____, but she [12]_____ in Rio de Janeiro. She [13]_____ in the evening, and she [14]_____ on the weekend.

2C Student B

1 Student A wants a roommate. Your friend, Jon, needs a room. Answer Student A's questions about Jon.

> Jon lives with his parents. He's a student. In his free time, he plays the guitar. He doesn't cook. He has a girlfriend. He loves music.

2 You want a roommate who has a job, doesn't stay home every night, and likes cats (you have one). Student A's friend, Helen, needs a room. Ask Student A questions. Is Helen a good roommate for you?

1 where / she / live ?
2 what / she / do ?
3 what / she / do / after work ?
4 she / stay home / every night ?
5 she / like / cats ?

bad   OK   good

3A Student B

1 Answer Student A's questions about Flora.

A *How often does Flora go to the movies?*
B *She goes to the movies three times a month.*

2 How often does Justin do these things? Ask Student A.

		Flora	Justin
1	go to the movies	three times a month	
2	cook in the evening	rarely	
3	play online games	never	
4	see his/her grandparents	every day	
5	go running	once a week	
6	listen to the radio	often	

3C Student B

Sophia and Sam are a couple. Ask Student A questions about Sophia, and answer Student A's questions about Sam. Find the following:

One thing that Sophia and Sam both love _____
One thing that Sophia and Sam both like _____
One thing that Sophia and Sam both hate _____

B *Does Sophia like getting takeout?*
A *Yes. She loves it!*

Sam

love ☺☺	like ☺	hate ☹
jazz	soccer	cook
go out for dinner	have a picnic	go shopping
walk the dog	watch TV	art
visit family	do yoga	read magazines

3D Student B

You want to meet Student A to go running this weekend. You're free at the following times. Ask and answer questions to find a time when you're both free.

B *Would you like to go running at 8:45 on Saturday morning?*
A *I'm sorry, I can't.*

SATURDAY
Free time
8:30 a.m. – 10:00 a.m.
1:30 p.m. – 2:30 p.m.
5:30 p.m. – 6:30 p.m.

SUNDAY
Free time
12:00 p.m. – 4:00 p.m.
7:30 p.m. – 9:30 p.m.

COMMUNICATION PRACTICE

4A Student B

1 Look at the pictures of Zak. Ask Student A questions about the missing information. Write the missing times or time expressions. Answer Student A's questions.

B *When does Zak walk the dog?*
A *He walks the dog at ...*

1 7:25

2 _____

3 9:00 – 5:30

4 _____

5 22:00 – 23:45

6 _____

7 Wednesday evenings

8 _____

9 Saturday mornings

10 _____

11 summer

12 _____

2 Compare with Student A. Do you have the same times?

4C Student B

1 Take turns describing your picture to Student A and listen to Student A's description. Find six differences between your picture and Student A's picture. Say what the people are doing.

A *In my picture, Clare and John are eating.*

B *In my picture, they're not eating. They're ...*

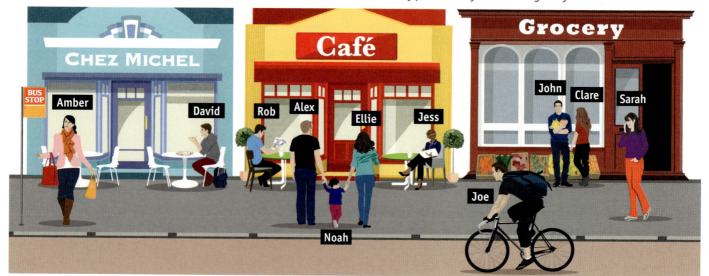

COMMUNICATION PRACTICE

5A Student B

1. Listen to Student A's description. Complete the sentences about Eric.
   1. Eric usually has _____ for breakfast, but today he's having _____.
   2. He usually wears _____, but today he's wearing _____.
   3. He usually goes to work _____, but today he's going _____.

2. Look at the pictures. Describe Emily to Student A. Use the words in the boxes to help you.

   | have wear go to work | pants and a sweater coffee a skirt and a blouse by subway by car tea |

   Emily usually ...   But today, she ...

3. Check your pictures and sentences with Student A. Do the sentences describe the pictures correctly?

5C Student B

1. Ask Student A about Artur and complete the chart. Answer Student A's questions about Alisha.

   B *Can Artur play a musical instrument?*
   A *No, he can't.*

Can he/she ...	Artur	Alisha
... speak a foreign language?		Yes (Italian)
... dance?		Yes (the Tango)
... play a musical instrument?		Yes (the drums)
... ride a horse?		No
... take good photos?		No
... cook?		Yes (Italian food)
... fix things?		Yes (computers)

5D Student B

1. You are a salesclerk in a department store. Student A is a customer. Begin the conversation with him/her. Use these sentences.

   - Yes, we do. I'll show you where they are.
   - It's 75 dollars.
   - Just a moment, I'll check. Yes. Here you are.
   - Yes, we take all credit cards.
   - Hello. Can I help you?
   - Yes, of course. The dressing rooms are over there.

2. You are a customer in a department store. Student A is a salesclerk. Student A begins the conversation. Ask him/her these questions.

   - And what colors are there?
   - Great. Thanks.
   - Yes, please. Do you have these pants in a size 28?
   - Thanks. Can I try them on?
   - Thanks. How much are they?
   - Where are the dressing rooms?

170

COMMUNICATION PRACTICE

6A Student B

1 Look at the picture and answer Student A's questions about his/her missing objects. You can only answer *yes* or *no*.

   A *Is there a mirror above the bed?*   B *No, there's not.*

2 Look at the objects in the box. Ask Student A questions to find out where they are.

   shoes   clock   shelves   lamp

6C Student B

1 A Look at the information about three cities. Answer Student A's questions..

  B Ask Student A for the missing information and write it in the chart.

   B *Is the mosque in Blue City beautiful?*   A *Yes. It's really beautiful.*

Blue City	Yellowtown	Greenville
mosque – beautiful?	beach – not very clean ✘	Old Town – pretty?
market – very busy ✔	restaurants – expensive?	cathedral – really beautiful ✔
museum – interesting?	local people – really friendly ✔	Central Park – clean?
art gallery – not very good ✘	hotels – nice?	river – really clean ✔
food and drinks – expensive?	museum – not interesting at all ✘	monuments – famous?

2 Decide which city you want to visit in pairs.

   A *I want to go to Yellowtown because it has really nice hotels.*   B *Yes, but the beach isn't very clean.*

IRREGULAR VERBS

Infinitive	Past simple	Past participle
be	was, were	been
become	became	become
begin	began	begun
bite	bit	bitten
break	broke	broken
bring	brought	brought
build	built	built
buy	bought	bought
choose	chose	chosen
come	came	come
cost	cost	cost
do	did	done
dream	dreamed/dreamt	dreamed/dreamt
forbid	forbade	forbidden
forget	forgot	forgotten
forgive	forgave	forgiven
get	got	gotten
give	gave	given
go	went	gone
grow	grew	grown
have	had	had
hear	heard	heard
hide	hid	hidden
hold	held	held
keep	kept	kept
know	knew	known
learn	learned	learned
leave	left	left
let	let	let
lose	lost	lost

Infinitive	Past simple	Past participle
make	made	made
meet	met	met
pay	paid	paid
put	put	put
read (/riːd/)	read (/red/)	read (/red/)
ride	rode	ridden
ring	rang	rung
rise	rose	risen
run	ran	run
say	said	said
see	saw	seen
sell	sold	sold
send	sent	sent
sleep	slept	slept
speak	spoke	spoken
spend	spent	spent
stand	stood	stood
steal	stole	stolen
stick	stuck	stuck
swim	swam	swum
take	took	taken
teach	taught	taught
tell	told	told
think	thought	thought
throw	threw	thrown
understand	understood	understood
wake	woke	woken
wear	wore	worn
win	won	won
write	wrote	written

American English

Personal Best

Workbook

A2
Elementary

Richmond

UNIT 1

You and me

1A LANGUAGE

GRAMMAR: The verb *be*

1 Choose the correct options to complete the sentences.

1. I *am / is / are* nineteen years old.
2. She *am / is / are* a teacher.
3. *Am / Is / Are* you from this country?
4. They *am not / isn't / aren't* at home.
5. We *am / is / are* all in the same class.
6. *Am / Is / Are* she English?
7. I *'m not / isn't / aren't* hungry.
8. It *am / is / are* nice to meet you.

2 Complete the sentences with the correct form of the verb *be*.

1. "Where's Malu?" "I don't know. She _____ here."
2. "Are you twenty?" "No, I _____ twenty-two."
3. My parents _____ in New York this week.
4. "Is Pablo your brother?" "No. He _____ my friend."
5. "Where are the children?" "They _____ at home. They're at school."
6. "_____ we all here?" "No, James is in the classroom."
7. You _____ a teacher. You're a student.
8. "_____ she Russian?" "No, she's Polish."

VOCABULARY: Numbers 1–1000, countries, and nationalities

3 Write the words or numbers.

1. 95 _____
2. twenty-one _____
3. 47 _____
4. two thousand _____
5. 12 _____
6. six hundred and thirty _____
7. 802 _____
8. eighty-five _____
9. 13 _____
10. fifteen _____

4 Match flags a–f with nationalities 1–6.

1. Swedish ___
2. Chinese ___
3. Australian ___
4. Argentinian ___
5. Vietnamese ___
6. Turkish ___

5 Complete the sentences with countries or nationalities.

1. My mom's from Japan. She's _____.
2. Our teacher is from _____. She's Canadian.
3. I'm from Ireland. I'm _____.
4. His best friend is from _____. She's Italian.
5. Marta is from Portugal. She's _____.
6. My dad's from the U.S. He's _____.
7. They are _____. They're from Brazil.
8. We are from Spain. We're _____.
9. Michel's _____. He's from France.
10. Wahid is from Egypt. He's _____.

PRONUNCIATION: Contractions of *be*

6 ▶1.1 Underline the contractions. Say the sentences. Listen, check, and repeat.

1. "Are you eighteen years old?" "No, I'm twenty."
2. "Where is Miguel?" "He's in a meeting."
3. This is the café. We're eating breakfast here.
4. Anna is my sister. She's an English teacher.
5. They're my friends. We are in the same class.
6. I know you. You're Sasha's brother.
7. "Is your car German?" "No, it's Italian."

SKILLS 1B

READING: Approaching a text

My trip with the orchestra

Hi! I'm Paula, and I'm from Portugal. I ¹_____ a student, but I'm also in a guitar orchestra for young people. Right now, I'm on a trip with the orchestra. We're ready to play concerts in London, Paris, and Rome! Here's my blog about my month of music.

WEEK 1

These are some of my friends from the orchestra. They ²_____ a lot of fun! Marina ³_____ nineteen, and Miguel is eighteen. They're my best friends. We usually go to the park together – we all like nature. We're in London right now, and there are lots of beautiful parks here.

WEEK 2

Our guitar teacher's name is Carlos, and he's very friendly. He is a great teacher – and he also cooks dinner for us every night. We all like his food very much.

WEEK 3

We ⁴_____ in Paris now, at a hotel downtown. There are a lot of English students in this hotel, so I practice my English every day. The orchestra plays music every morning until noon, and then we walk around the city. It's a really interesting place, and we see and do lots of things.

WEEK 4

We're in Rome now. It ⁵_____ an exciting city! Our concerts ⁶_____ in the evening, and we go shopping every day. My month of music is nearly finished. I'm happy because I want to see my family, but I'm sad because this trip is great.

1 Look at the title, headings, and pictures. Choose the best description for the text.
  a Someone who goes to music school every day.
  b Someone who travels with her orchestra for four weeks.
  c Someone who visits Rome on vacation.

2 Complete the text with the correct forms of the verb *be*.

3 Are the sentences true (T), false (F), or doesn't say (DS)?
  1 Paula is Portuguese. _____
  2 Her friend Marina is Spanish. _____
  3 There are nice parks in London. _____
  4 Carlos is a bad cook. _____
  5 There are no French students in the hotel in Paris. _____
  6 Miguel doesn't like Paris. _____
  7 Paula likes Rome. _____
  8 Marina and Miguel like shopping in Rome. _____

3

1C LANGUAGE

GRAMMAR: Possessive adjectives and 's for possession

1 Choose the correct options to complete the sentences.

1 My classmates and I all like ___ English teacher.
   a our   b his   c their
2 "What is your ___ name?" "Her name's Giulia."
   a sisters   b sisters'   c sister's
3 "Is this ___ key?" "Yes – it's mine."
   a my   b your   c her
4 Do you like ___ shoes? They're new!
   a Jame's   b James   c James'
5 "Where does Enrico live?" "___ house is over there."
   a Its   b His   c Your
6 "Is Emma at home?" "No. Her ___ car's not here."
   a parents   b parent's   c parents'
7 I have a white cat. ___ name is Snowy.
   a My   b Their   c Its
8 This store doesn't have ___ bags.
   a womens   b women's   c womens'

2 Complete the text with possessive adjectives.

I'm Juan, and this is a photo of ¹_____ class. You can see my best friend – ²_____ name's Marta – and ³_____ teacher. ⁴_____ name is Pedro, and he has two children. ⁵_____ names are Luisa and Carlos.

This is a photo of my house. Mom and I live here. It's a small house, but ⁶_____ garden is pretty big – we both like gardening! We have a cat, too – ⁷_____ name is Sooty because it is black and white. What about you? What are ⁸_____ friends and house like?

VOCABULARY: Personal objects

3 Match definitions 1–6 with objects a–f.

1 You can see your face in this. ___
2 You open a door with this. ___
3 You can talk to your friends with it. ___
4 You wear these on your hands when it's cold. ___
5 You need this when it rains. ___
6 You put your money in it. ___
   a umbrella
   b change purse
   c phone
   d gloves
   e key
   f mirror

4 Complete the words.

1 This is a p ___ ___ ___ ___ of me with my mom and my sister. We are on vacation!
2 You can buy a s ___ ___ ___ for your postcard at the post office.
3 What time is it? I don't have a w ___ ___ ___ .
4 When I walk at night, I take a f ___ ___ ___ ___ ___ ___ ___ ___ to help me see.
5 My name and address are on my i ___ ___ ___ ___ ___ ___ c ___ ___ ___ .
6 I eat a lot of c ___ ___ ___ . My mom says it's bad for my teeth.
7 I can't read this without my g ___ ___ ___ ___ ___ .
8 We can't have c ___ ___ ___ ___ ___ g ___ ___ during class.

PRONUNCIATION: Sentence stress

5 ▶ 1.2 Listen and repeat the sentences. Underline the stressed words in each sentence. Listen again, check, and repeat.

1 What's in his wallet?
2 Here are your books.
3 My tablet is on the chair.
4 What's her name?
5 Their house is new.
6 Where are my tissues?

SKILLS 1D

SPEAKING: Asking for and giving personal information

1 ▶1.3 Listen to the conversation. Which sentence is correct?

- A Miguel is at home.
- B Miguel is on the phone.
- C Miguel is at the gym.

2 ▶1.3 Listen again. Complete the sentences.

1 What's your f_____ name?
2 And what's your _____?
3 Do you have an _____ address, Miguel?
4 And what's your _____ number, please?
5 What's your a_____?
6 OK. What's your z_____?

3 ▶1.3 Listen again and complete the form below.

4 ▶1.3 Does the receptionist ask for clarification for Miguel's information? Listen again and write A, B, or C for 1–6. There may be more than one answer.

- A Yes, she asks, "How do you spell that (please)?"
- B Yes, she asks Miguel to repeat information.
- C No, she doesn't ask for clarification.

1 first name _____
2 last name _____
3 e-mail address _____
4 cell phone number _____
5 address _____
6 zip code _____

5 ▶1.4 Look at the information on the form below. Listen and check if it is correct. Ask for clarification and make sure you use polite intonation.

SUPERFIT GYM Date: _____

CLIENT INFORMATION
First name:
....
Last name:
....

CONTACT DETAILS
E-mail:
..................@starmail.com
Phone number:
917
Address:
8 .... Street
Zip code:
....

SUPERFIT GYM Date: _____

CLIENT INFORMATION
First name:
MARIA
Last name:
PALMA

CONTACT DETAILS
E-mail:
palma90@newmail.com
Phone number:
215-555-0079
Address:
527 Queen Road
Zip code:
19147

5

1 REVIEW and PRACTICE

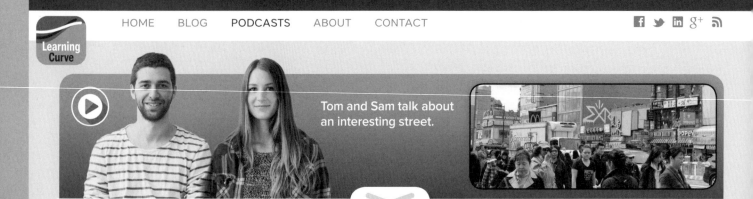

LISTENING

1 ▶ 1.5 Listen to the podcast about an interesting street. Read the sentences. Are they true (T) or false (F)?

1 Roosevelt Avenue is in the U.S. _____
2 It's interesting because it's a very international street. _____
3 Jacob's store sells stamps. _____
4 His mother is from Ireland. _____
5 Mr. Deng is Vietnamese. _____
6 He cooks and serves food. _____
7 Maria is Portuguese. _____
8 Anna is from India. _____

2 ▶ 1.5 Listen again. Complete the sentences with the numbers in the box. There are four numbers you don't need.

| 2 | 3 | 4 | 53 | 63 |
| 73 | 118 | 122 | 180 |

1 Jacob's store sells _____ different kinds of candy.
2 People from _____ different countries live in the neighborhood.
3 Mr. Deng has _____ restaurants.
4 Maria has _____ children.
5 Anna has _____ sisters.

READING

1 Read the blog on page 7 about an international home. Write the people's nationalities.

1 Suki _____
2 Lucja _____
3 Ryan _____
4 Simona _____
5 Marco _____

2 Circle the countries in the blog and underline the personal objects.

3 Are the sentences true (T), false (F), or doesn't say (DS)?

1 Suki is from France. _____
2 Five people live in Suki's apartment. _____
3 Lucja speaks English well. _____
4 Suki is eighteen years old. _____
5 Ryan is a student. _____
6 Ryan works in a store in Paris. _____
7 Simona doesn't like the weather in Brazil. _____
8 Simona's family lives in Brazil. _____
9 Marco has a job in Paris. _____
10 Marco is Suki's boyfriend. _____

REVIEW and PRACTICE | 1

HOME **BLOG** PODCASTS ABOUT CONTACT

Guest blogger Penny writes about people living in another country.

AN INTERNATIONAL HOME

All around the world, young people live and study away from their own homes. But what's it like living with people from other countries? I asked Suki, a photography student. Suki's from Vietnam, but she lives in France now. Here's what she says about life in her international home.

I live in an apartment in Paris with four other people. We're all from different countries, but we can all speak English really well. Our apartment is very friendly, and, of course, it has a great international atmosphere!

Lucja is from Poland, and she's eighteen years old. She is a student, like me. She wants to be a dentist, but she really loves candy! Lucja's a very happy person – I like her a lot. Here's a photo of her looking happy.

Ryan is twenty-five years old, and he is from Ireland. He works in a café near our apartment. He likes shopping, and he loves shopping for clothes. Here's a photo of him wearing his favorite sunglasses. He thinks they are very cool!

Simona is from Brazil. She's twenty-one years old, and she's a nurse. She doesn't like the weather here – she is always cold! I think she is unhappy because she can't see her family back home very often, and she misses her son. Here's Simona with her favorite umbrella – she takes it everywhere she goes!

Marco is from Italy. He's a student, too, but he wants to be a model. He's very handsome, isn't he? He's 23 years old, and he likes cars, soccer, and looking in the mirror!

Who do you live with? Tell us about them and where you live. Don't forget to send us some photographs, too!

7

UNIT 2 Work and play

2A LANGUAGE

GRAMMAR: Simple present: affirmative and negative

1 Choose the correct options to complete the sentences.

1 He _____ a taxi every evening.
 a drives   b drive
 c don't drive

2 My sister _____ English – she teaches math.
 a teach   b doesn't teach
 c teaches

3 I like my job, but it _____ very well.
 a doesn't pay   b pays
 c pay

4 On the weekend, I'm a tour guide. I _____ tourists around my city.
 a doesn't take   b takes
 c take

5 I speak French, but I _____ German.
 a don't speak   b speaks
 c speak

6 My mom _____ in a restaurant. She serves food.
 a work   b works
 c don't work

2 Complete the e-mail with the correct simple present form of the verbs in parentheses.

Hi Malin,

How are you? I am very busy right now. I ¹_____ (work) a lot of hours every day.

We ²_____ (have) a new teacher at school – Mrs. Black. She ³_____ (teach) us English and French. She's very funny – everyone ⁴_____ (like) her. Mrs. Black loves movies, and we ⁵_____ (watch) a lot of interesting videos in her class. She ⁶_____ (live) near here, though – she drives from Boston every day!

Mom and dad say "hello"! They are busy, too. The restaurant is very popular, and they ⁷_____ (serve) food and drink all day, every day!

Write soon,

Tamara

VOCABULARY: Jobs and job verbs

3 Order the letters to make words for jobs.

1 My mom's a TRODCO. She works in a hospital.
 _____

2 I'm a student, but on Friday nights I'm a GISREN with my band.
 _____

3 Ask a CAIMNECH to look at your car.
 _____

4 You must be good at math to work as an TONCANACUT.
 _____

5 I love traveling, so I want to be a THIGLF NETTANDTA.
 _____

6 I need to go to the STINTED. My teeth hurt.
 _____

7 My sister works as a TOESCIRENPIT in a hotel.
 _____

8 This light is broken. I have to call an CAINCLEETRI.
 _____

4 Complete the sentences with job verbs.

1 Julio is a waiter. He _____ food in a restaurant.
2 My hairdresser _____ my hair every month.
3 Her aunt is a salesclerk. She _____ computers in a big store.
4 He always _____ a suit to work because he's a lawyer.
5 Sonia is a tour guide. She _____ tourists with their questions.
6 His brother is a famous chef. He _____ food in the best hotel in Rome.

PRONUNCIATION: -s and -es endings

5 ▶ 2.1 Listen and circle the sound that you hear at the end of the underlined verb. Listen again, check, and repeat.

1 Suki works in a restaurant.	/s/	/z/	/ɪz/
2 Anna watches TV every day.	/s/	/z/	/ɪz/
3 Sally helps her brother with his homework.	/s/	/z/	/ɪz/
4 Jean Paul drives an Italian car.	/s/	/z/	/ɪz/
5 Ester really likes chocolate.	/s/	/z/	/ɪz/
6 Roberto lives in Argentina.	/s/	/z/	/ɪz/
7 Max teaches science.	/s/	/z/	/ɪz/
8 Turgay sells shoes.	/s/	/z/	/ɪz/

8

Skills 2B

LISTENING: Listening for names, places, days, and times

1 ▶ 2.2 Listen to the conversation between two friends. Which names and places do you hear?

  1 a Janine   b Jenny   c Joan
  2 a Donna   b Donald   c Danny
  3 a Mateo's   b Maria's   c Marco's
  4 a Boston   b Houston   c Stockton
  5 a Vicky   b Vinny   c Ricky

2 ▶ 2.2 Complete the sentences with *in*, *on*, or *at*. Then listen again and check.

  1 Vanessa plays tennis ____ seven o'clock.
  2 She eats pizza ____ the Italian restaurant.
  3 ____ Thursday night, she studies.
  4 She is always ____ Boston on Friday evenings.
  5 Paul watches TV ____ Saturday evening.
  6 Paul's favorite TV show starts ____ eight o'clock.

3 Match the words to make activities.

  1 play   ____   a friends
  2 read   ____   b to music
  3 meet   ____   c the guitar
  4 spend time   ____   d English
  5 go out   ____   e a movie
  6 see   ____   f with my family
  7 study   ____   g for dinner
  8 listen   ____   h the newspaper

4 Complete the sentences with six of the activities from exercise 3. Use the correct form of the verbs. Use affirmative and negative forms.

  1 She's the singer in the band, and she also _____.
  2 I _____ at home. I don't have a favorite group.
  3 They _____ every day. They know a lot about the world.
  4 She _____ at the new language school downtown.
  5 We _____ every week. We really like Italian restaurants.
  6 Now that I am in college, I _____ except on vacation.

5 ▶ 2.3 Read the sentences. Underline the words that only have the sound /ə/. Then listen and check.

  1 Do you like music?
  2 My sister's a teacher.
  3 I want to play tennis!
  4 What do you do in your free time?
  5 He goes to school on Saturday morning.
  6 Where is the movie theater?

9

2C LANGUAGE

GRAMMAR: Simple present: questions

1 Complete the sentences with the words in the box.

| what | do | who | does (x 2) | how |
| when | where | don't (x 2) | | |

1 _____ you play soccer?
2 "Does she work here?" "Yes, she _____."
3 _____ do you go after work?
4 "Do they like dogs?" "No, they _____."
5 _____ does he live with?
6 _____ does class start?
7 _____ your father speak Italian?
8 "Do you know Lisa?" "No, we _____."
9 _____ do they do on the weekend?
10 _____ do you say this word?

2 Order the words to make questions.

1 does / study / where / he / Turkish
   _____?
2 Vietnam / you / come from / do
   _____?
3 she / a cat / does / have
   _____?
4 with / they / who / do / go out
   _____?
5 at / do / start work / eight / we
   _____?
6 you / do / why / to school / drive
   _____?
7 does / fix / where / she / cars
   _____?
8 suit / wear / he / a / does
   _____?

PRONUNCIATION: Auxiliary do/does in questions

3 Look at the pictures. Use the prompts to write questions about Carla.

1 where/live?
   _____
2 how/work?
   _____
3 when/home?
   _____
4 do/study/evening?
   _____
5 what/weekends?
   _____
6 who/movies?
   _____

4 ▶2.4 Say the questions. How do we say *do* and *does*? Listen, check, and repeat.

1 Do you like pizza?
2 Does he live with his parents?
3 What do you do on the weekend?
4 Do they speak Spanish?
5 Where does he work?
6 When do you watch TV?
7 Does your sister teach yoga?
8 Who do you spend time with in the evening?

SKILLS 2D

WRITING: Opening and closing an informal e-mail

Hey Lucy,

How are things with you? Do you like your new home in New York?

Here in Madrid, everything is fine. I have a new roommate. She is really nice and friendly, but I often think of you and wish you were here! Her name is Keira, and she's from New Zealand. She's a good cook, but she doesn't make great chocolate cake like you!

I have a new part-time job. I'm a tour guide – I take people around Madrid and show them the sights. I work every afternoon, from 2 p.m. till 6 or 7 p.m. I really like my job, but I don't have a lot of free time right now! You can see me working in this photo.

In the evenings, I am pretty tired, but I sometimes play tennis with Keira. On weekends, I usually go to the movies or go shopping.

Take care,
María

1 Read María's e-mail then look at the phrases below. Are they opening (O) or closing (C) phrases?

1 Hi ____
2 Write soon ____
3 See you soon ____
4 Hello ____
5 Hi Marta ____
6 Love, Freddie XXX ____

2 Find and underline the connectors in the e-mail.

3 Choose the correct connectors.

1 I really like coffee, *and / but* I don't like tea at all.
2 Is that your mother, *and / or* is it your sister?
3 I go to school, *and / so* I also have extra English classes.
4 I'm from Spain, *but / and* I now live in Mexico.
5 I have two sisters: Vanessa *and / or* Sally.
6 Are you a teacher *or / but* a student?

4 Complete the e-mail with *and*, *but*, or *or*.

Hi Samantha,

I'm on vacation in Granada in Spain. Our vacation is really fun ¹_____ exciting, ²_____ I wish you were here. I think it's the perfect place for you. You can choose to go to the beach ³_____ the mountains. The food ⁴_____ drinks are delicious, ⁵_____ people have lunch too late! They don't eat until 3 o'clock!

I will call you soon ⁶_____ write another e-mail.

Bye,
Clare

5 Write an e-mail to a friend in another country. Use *and*, *but*, and *or* to connect your ideas. Include:

- an informal opening phrase
- information about your home, friends, and free time
- an informal closing phrase.

11

2 REVIEW and PRACTICE

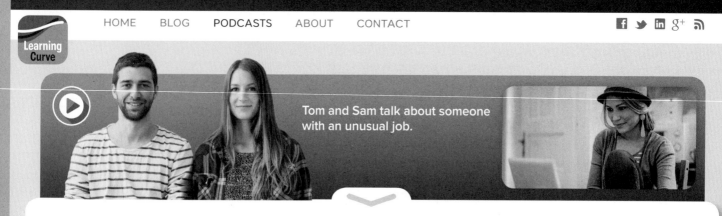

LISTENING

1 ▶ 2.5 Listen to the podcast about someone with an interesting job. Choose the correct answers.

1 Which sentence about Arabella is true?
   a She doesn't like going to the movies.
   b Her hobby is also her job.
   c She reads a lot of newspapers.
2 What is Arabella's job?
   a She sells tickets at a movie theater.
   b She's the manager of a magazine.
   c She writes about movies.
3 What does Arabella say about Luke?
   a He really likes movies.
   b He is her friend.
   c He doesn't talk a lot.

2 ▶ 2.5 Listen again. Complete the sentences with one or two words.

1 Arabella really loves her _____.
2 She writes about movies for _____ and magazines.
3 She goes to the movies _____ times a week.
4 She really likes horror _____.
5 After she sees a movie, she likes to _____ it.
6 She also writes about _____.

3 ▶ 2.5 Order the words to make questions. Listen again and check your answers.

1 go / do / you / every night / to the movies ?
   _____

2 what kind / like / you / do / of movies ?
   _____

3 you / take / with you / a friend / do ?
   _____

4 have / you / do / another job ?
   _____

READING

1 Read the blog on page 13 about work and free time. Answer the questions.

1 What is Tom Fletcher's job?
2 Does Tom think we have a good work-life balance?
3 What does Tom think we need to spend more time doing?

2 Does Tom say the things below? Choose Yes or No.

1	Many people start work at seven o'clock.	Yes	No
2	People work more hours in winter.	Yes	No
3	Tom has his lunch at home.	Yes	No
4	Many people always feel tired.	Yes	No
5	Playing the guitar can make you feel good.	Yes	No
6	Meeting friends is a good idea.	Yes	No
7	We have to all walk for fifteen minutes every day.	Yes	No
8	More free time is also good for your family.	Yes	No

3 Circle the free-time activities in the blog.

REVIEW and PRACTICE 2

HOME | **BLOG** | PODCASTS | ABOUT | CONTACT

Guest blogger Kate writes about ideas for a work-life balance.

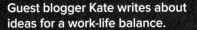

Work or life?

Today, lots of people work or study for more than 50 hours a week. We don't have much free time during the week. But it's important to have a "work-life balance" and to have some time away from work and studying. What can we do to make sure we don't work too much? Here are some ideas from life coach, Tom Fletcher.

People work really hard these days. Think about it – most of us read our work e-mails before breakfast! Then we work until seven o'clock. In the winter, we probably don't see the sun! Sixty percent of us take work home, too – and check our work e-mails late at night.

This is what a lot of people tell me about their day: "I get up at six o'clock, eat lunch at my desk, and go home at ten o'clock at night. I don't have time to go to a restaurant or to meet friends. I don't spend time with my family either – I'm always too busy. I want to relax, but there's not enough time during the day. I'm always tired, and I don't really enjoy my life right now."

This isn't good for our minds or bodies. You need to make time for life, because it's important to do things that you enjoy. Listen to music, play the guitar, read a book or go to the movies – these are things that make you feel good. And when you feel good, you can also work better.

Free-time activities don't need a lot of time – it's easy to make small changes to your day. Do you eat your lunch at your desk? Why not go out to a café – it's much more fun! Try to meet friends every day. Go for a fifteen-minute walk together. It makes you feel great and gives you more energy!

13

UNIT 3

People in my life

3A LANGUAGE

GRAMMAR: Adverbs and frequency expressions

1 Order the words to make sentences.

1 always / is / your sister / late for school
   _____.

2 together / eats dinner / our family / once a week
   _____.

3 grandparents / sees / his / he / twice a month
   _____.

4 because / play tennis / I / never / I don't like it
   _____.

5 breakfast / they / eat / sometimes / a big
   _____.

6 in the kitchen / a day / helps my mother / my brother / three times
   _____.

2 Complete the conversation with adverbs and frequency expressions.

Anas	What do you ¹u_____ during the summer vacation?
Sara	I travel to the U.S. ²o_____ a year.
Anas	You're so lucky!
Sara	Well, my family lives there, and I don't ³o_____ see them. But I visit my cousins ⁴t_____ a month because they live near me. What about you?
Anas	I stay home ⁵e_____ year.
Sara	Really? Isn't that boring?
Anas	Not at all! I work in a café three ⁶t_____ a week, and I see my friends every day.

VOCABULARY: Family

3 Match the two parts of the sentences.

1 My aunt ____
2 My mother-in-law ____
3 My nephew ____
4 My grandparents ____
5 My niece ____
6 My sister-in-law ____

a is my husband's sister.
b is my brother's son.
c is my mother's sister.
d is my wife's mother.
e are my parents' mother and father.
f is my sister's daughter.

4 Complete the family words.

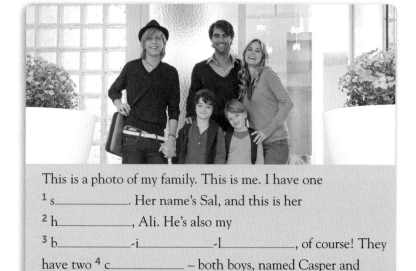

This is a photo of my family. This is me. I have one ¹s_____. Her name's Sal, and this is her ²h_____, Ali. He's also my ³b_____-i_____-l_____, of course! They have two ⁴c_____ – both boys, named Casper and John – who are my ⁵n_____. My ⁶f_____ took the photo. His brother, Fred, is my favorite ⁷u_____!

PRONUNCIATION: Sentence stress

5 ▶3.1 Read the sentences. Stress the adverbs and frequency expressions. Listen, check, and repeat.

1 He sometimes visits his cousin.
2 We're never late.
3 I study English every day.
4 I see my nephew once a week.
5 We often eat Chinese food.
6 I usually go to the park with my niece.

14

SKILLS 3B

READING: Scanning a text

VACATIONS WITH A DIFFERENCE!

IT'S VACATION TIME! READ ABOUT OUR ACTIVE VACATIONS
WHICH ONE DO YOU LIKE BEST?

A PONY HIKING

Our pony hiking vacations are very popular. On these vacations, you stay in a quiet hotel in a beautiful place. Then you get up early and go pony hiking until 3 p.m. with one of our friendly guides. You also learn all about pony care.

C TAKE A BREAK – WITH A YOGA VACATION

Are you busy at work? Are you always tired? Relax and spend time with other people who love yoga. You stay in a beautiful small house near the sea. In the morning, you practice yoga, and go swimming in the sea. In the afternoon and evening, you eat our healthy food (it's also delicious!).

B SINGING IN SUMMER!

Do you love music? Then this vacation is for you. On this special vacation, you sing in a group every morning for two hours. Then, in the afternoon, you give group concerts in the town center. In the evening, you relax and sometimes go dancing, too. It's a lot of fun!

D ARTS AND CRAFTS

Our arts and crafts vacation is for people who love to make things. Every morning you learn a different craft, and in the afternoon, you go on trips to visit different artists. In the evening, you show the other students your work. It's a fun vacation, and it's interesting, too!

1 Scan the text. On which vacation do you:

1 eat delicious food? _____
2 dance in the evenings? _____
3 stay in a hotel? _____
4 learn different crafts? _____

2 Are the sentences true (T), false (F), or doesn't say (DS)?

1 On the pony hiking vacation, you go riding with a guide. _____
2 You can go swimming in the evening on the pony hiking vacation. _____
3 You meet people from different countries on the singing vacation. _____
4 On the singing vacation, you can relax in the evenings. _____
5 You buy and cook your own food on the yoga vacation. _____

6 On the yoga vacation, you stay near the sea. _____
7 On the arts and crafts vacation, other people can look at your work. _____
8 You make different things in the afternoon on the arts and crafts vacation. _____

3 Complete the sentences with *also* or *too*.

1 These vacations sound good! I like the yoga vacation and the singing vacation, _____.
2 I want to go on the pony hiking vacations and I _____ want to go on the yoga vacation.
3 I like ponies, and I _____ like quiet hotels.
4 On the arts and crafts vacation, you make art, and you look at other people's work, _____.
5 Singing is fun, and it's relaxing, _____.
6 Yoga is interesting, and it's _____ very good for you.

15

3C LANGUAGE

GRAMMAR: *love, like, hate, enjoy, don't mind* + noun/*-ing* form

1 Complete the text with the *-ing* form of the verbs in parentheses.

I love ¹_____ (live) with my family! We're all very happy. My dad enjoys ²_____ (drive) his taxi for work every day. My mom's very busy, so I don't mind ³_____ (make) breakfast for my little sister and ⁴_____ (take) her to the park sometimes. My brother, Pat, loves ⁵_____ (run) in the park, and he really likes ⁶_____ (swim) in the outside pool there – but he hates ⁷_____ (go) to school! On the weekend, we all enjoy ⁸_____ (be) together. Sometimes I like to be alone though. I love ⁹_____ (sit) with a book or ¹⁰_____ (plan) my future!

2 Complete the sentences with *love* / *don't like* / *doesn't like* / *hate* / *enjoy* / *don't mind* + *-ing* form of the verbs in the box.

| study | help | meet | work | spend |
| play | go | relax | watch | eat |

1 Do you _____ time with your family on the weekend? ☺
2 I _____ vegetables, but I like French fries more! ☹
3 My sister _____ math and never does her homework. ☹☹
4 Do you _____ in the evening after work? ☺
5 We _____ our friends for coffee in the new café in town. ☺☺
6 Jaime _____ to the dentist, so he doesn't go very often. ☹☹
7 His uncle makes cars. He _____ in a factory. ☹
8 They _____ their mom with the shopping and cooking. ☺
9 I _____ movies at home, but I go to the movie theater every week. ☹
10 Does your brother _____ online games? ☺☺

VOCABULARY: Activities (2)

3 Order the letters to make words for activities.

1 OG PSHOPNIG
_____

2 OG OT A LLAGYRE
_____

3 LYAP HET LINVIO
_____

4 OG GLIBWON
_____

5 OD GOYA
_____

6 HEAV A CINCIP
_____

7 APLY LOVELYBLLA
_____

8 ISITV STERILAVE
_____

4 Complete the sentences with the correct verbs.

1 What great weather! Do you want to _____ a barbecue?
2 When it rains on vacation, I like to _____ to museums.
3 I never _____ golf – I think it's a boring game.
4 My girlfriend loves to _____ swimming, but I hate the water!
5 I don't have time to cook, so I often _____ a takeout for dinner.
6 I want to _____ dancing tonight. There's a great DJ playing!
7 Do you want to _____ bike riding on the weekend?
8 His niece wants to learn to _____ karate next year.

PRONUNCIATION: *-ing* forms

5 ▶3.2 Say the sentences. How do we say the *-ing* forms? Listen, check, and repeat.

1 I don't mind playing tennis.
2 We love visiting our grandmother.
3 I don't like being late.
4 I love reading stories.
5 I like running.
6 I hate watching TV.
7 I don't mind going to school.
8 I enjoy playing sports.

SKILLS 3D

SPEAKING: Accepting or declining an invitation

1 Look at the clocks and write the times.

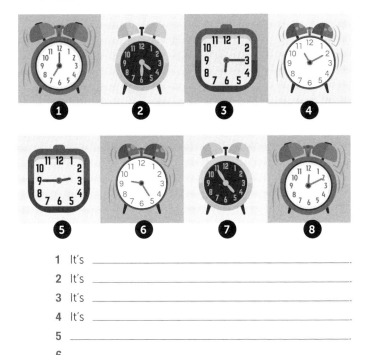

1 It's _____.
2 It's _____.
3 It's _____.
4 It's _____.
5 _____.
6 _____.
7 _____.
8 _____.

2 ▶ 3.3 Listen to the conversation between two friends. Are the sentences true or false?

1	Pablo suggests going for a walk.	True	False
2	Sara accepts Pablo's invitation for tonight.	True	False
3	Sara has to visit her grandfather.	True	False
4	Pablo suggests tomorrow morning.	True	False
5	They agree to meet at one o'clock.	True	False

3 ▶ 3.3 Complete the lines from the conversation with the words in the box. Then listen again and check.

how	let's	can't	time
say	about	plans	want

1 Do you have _____ after work today?
2 Do you _____ to go to the movies with me?
3 Tonight? Oh, I'm sorry, I _____.
4 What _____ tomorrow?
5 _____ about having lunch with me?
6 Great, _____ go together.
7 What _____ is good for you?
8 Let's _____ one o'clock.

4 Match 1–5 with a–e to make conversations.

1 Do you want to come to my birthday party on Saturday? _____
2 Would you like to come to the game with me? I've got two tickets. _____
3 How about going to the new burger restaurant together? _____
4 Do you want to have coffee together later? _____
5 Are you free for lunch today? _____

a I'd love to, but I don't eat meat. Sorry!
b Cool! I love soccer.
c Sure!
d Yes, I'd love to!
e Saturday? I'm sorry, I can't.

5 ▶ 3.4 Listen and check. Then say if the people accept (A) or decline (D) the invitations in each conversation.

1 _____
2 _____
3 _____
4 _____
5 _____

6 ▶ 3.4 Listen again and repeat the conversations in exercise 4. Copy the intonation to sound enthusiastic or sorry.

17

3 REVIEW and PRACTICE

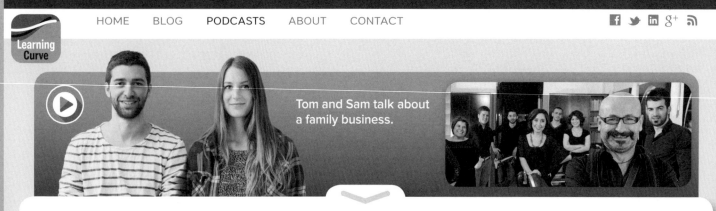

LISTENING

1 ▶ 3.5 Listen to the podcast about a family business called "Swish." Number a–h in the order you hear them (1–8).

- a brother _____
- b sisters _____
- c mother _____
- d grandmother _____
- e grandfather _____
- f cousins _____
- g sister-in-law _____
- h aunts _____

2 ▶ 3.5 Listen again and choose the correct answers.

1 Why do people enjoy going to Swish?
  a The haircuts are very cheap.
  b The hairdressers are friendly.
  c There's a nice atmosphere.

2 How many family members work at the hairdresser?
  a ten
  b eleven
  c thirteen

3 How many aunts does Mila have?
  a two
  b three
  c four

4 What does Mila do at Swish?
  a She cuts hair.
  b She makes coffee.
  c She does lots of different things.

5 Does the family enjoy working together?
  a sometimes
  b usually
  c always

6 Why are there problems sometimes?
  a because of money
  b because of customers
  c because they are busy

READING

1 Read the blog on page 19 about spending time with your family. Write R (Roberto), M (Mariella), or B (both). Who:

1 doesn't like playing golf? _____
2 is busy at work? _____
3 likes going out with friends? _____
4 doesn't enjoy going dancing? _____
5 doesn't like shopping? _____
6 goes cycling three times a month? _____

2 Are the sentences true (T) or false (F)?

1 Roberto doesn't like music. _____
2 Mariella and Roberto hardly ever talk together. _____
3 Mariella plays golf with her friends. _____
4 Roberto likes playing golf with his daughter. _____
5 Roberto has a lot of free time. _____
6 Mariella and Roberto sometimes ride their bikes to the beach. _____
7 Mariella talks to her father about school. _____
8 Roberto enjoys going bike riding with Mariella. _____

3 Circle the adverbs and expressions of frequency in the blog.

REVIEW and PRACTICE 3

HOME BLOG PODCASTS ABOUT CONTACT

Guest blogger Simon writes about how a father and a daughter spend time together.

Family time

In today's busy world, it's not always easy for families to spend time together. So why not try doing your mother's, father's, son's, or daughter's hobby with them? Read about how Mariella and her dad, Roberto, enjoy some free time together.

Mariella

My dad plays golf three times a week. He's always at the golf course. I don't know why! I don't think it's a great sport – you don't run, there's no music, and I don't like the clothes people wear!

I don't see my dad very often, and sometimes I don't know what to talk to him about. That's why I like coming here together, because there's always something to talk about – where the golf ball is going, for example! When we're at home, I'm usually on my phone talking to friends. But I never look at my phone when we play golf!

I play golf with Dad about once a week. I don't really like it very much, but I like being with him, and I know he enjoys it, too.

Roberto

I have a very busy job, and I hardly ever have free time. But Mariella doesn't talk to me often. She has a lot of friends, and she enjoys going out with them. And she never stops talking on her phone! She loves going to clubs, too – but it's not my favorite thing! It's probably a bit boring to go out with your father. So it's great that Mariella plays golf with me. It's very special.

Mariella loves bike riding, so we also go bike riding together three times a month. Mariella always decides where to go. Sometimes we take our bikes to the beach, and sometimes to the hills. We often talk – usually about things like school or work. Sometimes we talk about our favorite music. I'm happy to do Mariella's hobby with her. But I hope she never asks me to go shopping with her. I hate going shopping!

UNIT 4 Home and away

4A LANGUAGE

GRAMMAR: Prepositions of time

1 Complete the sentences with the words in the box.

in (x2)   on (x3)   to   at   from

1 _____ Friday nights, I usually get takeout.
2 The bank is open _____ 10 a.m. to 4 p.m.
3 School is always closed _____ August.
4 _____ the winter, I don't go out very often.
5 We study a lot _____ the weekend.
6 I'm always tired _____ Monday mornings.
7 Where were you _____ midnight last night?
8 The outdoor swimming pool is open from May _____ October.

2 Complete the text with prepositions of time.

A typical day? Well, I usually get up ¹_____ 7 a.m., but ²_____ the summer it's lighter, so I get up earlier – maybe 6:30 a.m. I have a job in a café – I serve food to customers.
I work ³_____ 10 a.m. ⁴_____ 6 p.m. every day during the week – ⁵_____ Monday ⁶_____ Friday. After work, ⁷_____ 6 p.m., I usually meet my friends. ⁸_____ Friday nights, we go to a restaurant or to the movies. ⁹_____ July, the café is closed for one month, so I don't work at all. It's also closed ¹⁰_____ New Year's. Then, my typical day is very different!

VOCABULARY: Daily routine verbs

3 Put verbs a–g in order (1–8) to make a typical day.

a get home _____
b finish work _____
c have dinner _____
d go to bed _____
e have breakfast _____
f go to sleep _____
g get up _____
h go to work _____

4 Order the letters to make daily routine verbs.

1 I **egt deresds** after a big breakfast.
2 Do you watch TV before you **og ot loshoc**?
3 My brother often doesn't **veah clunh** because he's busy.
4 Yolanda likes to **kwae pu** early and read a magazine.
5 On Sunday, before I **teg pu**, I have a cup of coffee.
6 Does he **akte a roshew** every morning?
7 Our mom sometimes **saket a hatb** before bed.
8 When they **hsifni closho**, they play in the park.

PRONUNCIATION: Sentence stress

5 ▶ 4.1 Read the sentences. Which words are stressed? Listen, check, and repeat.

1 I get up at eleven o'clock.
2 I go to school from nine o'clock to three o'clock.
3 We have breakfast at 7:30.
4 He rides his bike to work in the summer.
5 I play soccer on Saturday afternoons.
6 She wakes up at eight.

20

SKILLS 4B

LISTENING: Listening for the main idea

1 ▶ 4.2 Listen to a conversation about Hong Kong. Check (✓) the different types of weather you hear.

a ____

b ____

c ____

d ____

e ____

f ____

2 ▶ 4.2 Listen again. Are the sentences true (T) or false (F)?

1 The weather is always the same in Hong Kong. ____
2 Fiona doesn't like hot weather. ____
3 Fiona is a student. ____
4 It never rains in Hong Kong. ____
5 Typhoons bring bad weather. ____

3 Complete the weather words for a–f in exercise 1.

a s_____g
b s_____y
c r_____g
d f_____y
e w_____y
f c_____y

4 Order the letters to make seasons. Which words from exercise 3 describe the weather in your country in each season?

1 RETWIN _____
2 GRINPS _____
3 LALF _____
4 REMUMS _____

5 ▶ 4.3 Read the sentences. Underline the words which you think will be stressed. Listen and check.

1 What's the climate like there?
2 There are four seasons.
3 The weather is too hot for me.
4 It always rains here!
5 Is Hong Kong a beautiful city?

21

4C LANGUAGE

GRAMMAR: Present continuous

1 Choose the correct options to complete the sentences.

1 I ___ a great time in New York.
   a has   b having   c 'm having

2 "Where's Peter?" "He ___ his mother right now."
   a 's helping   b helps   c are helping

3 "Are we eating lunch here?" "No, we ___."
   a don't   b 're not   c 's not

4 Where ___ you going right now?
   a is   b are   c do

5 I'm ___ enjoying this movie.
   a doesn't b not   c no

6 Are you ___ to the party on Friday?
   a come   b comes   c coming

7 Laila's ___ tonight, so she's not here.
   a work   b works   c working

8 ___ they having a karate class today?
   a Do   b Are   c Is

9 "Is he listening to the radio?" "No, he ___."
   a is   b doesn't   c 's not

10 They ___ going to clubs downtown this week.
   a 're not b not   c don't

2 Order the words to make statements and questions.

1 in / we / the classroom / sitting / are / now
   _____.

2 their vacation / Brazil / aren't / they / spending / in
   _____.

3 today / are / enjoying / the children / school
   _____?

4 she / right now / listening / 's not
   _____.

5 visiting / you / this week / are / new places
   _____?

6 right / is / now / snowing / it
   _____?

7 walking / today / not / the dog / I'm
   _____.

8 camping / he / is / this year / going
   _____.

PRONUNCIATION: Consonant-to-vowel linking

3 ▶ 4.4 Underline the words that are linked. Listen, check, and repeat.

1 What are you doing tomorrow?
2 I'm going away next weekend.
3 She's eating her breakfast.
4 It's not very warm today.
5 I'm getting up late tomorrow.
6 He's asking his teacher.

4 Write sentences to describe what the people (1–8) in the picture are doing.

22

SKILLS 4D

WRITING: Describing a photo

Hey Rob,

How are you? I'm having a great time in London. I'm going to summer school – I love learning English! The weather's not very hot, and it rains a lot, but ¹_____'s good weather for learning and sightseeing.

I'm really busy – there's so much to do! Classes start at 9 a.m. and ²_____ finish at 1 p.m. I usually get up early and go for a walk before breakfast. I study English with the other students all morning, and then ³_____ stop for lunch. After lunch, we all go downtown to see the sights. In the evening, we have dinner together. Then we go to the park or play soccer.

I'm sending you a few photos. In this photo, I'm playing soccer with my new friend, George. George is from Serbia – ⁴_____'s really good at sports. This is a photo of my classroom with my English teacher, Joanna. ⁵_____'s really funny, and I enjoy her classes. Here's a photo of my classmates in the park – ⁶_____'s a beautiful place to relax.

Are you in London right now? Can we meet some afternoon?

See you soon,

Fernando

1 Read Fernando's e-mail. Complete 1–6 with the correct pronouns.

2 Number a–e in the order Fernando does the things (1–5).

  a describes his daily routine _____
  b asks Rob to meet him _____
  c talks about the weather _____
  d describes some photographs _____
  e asks Rob a friendly question _____

3 Complete the sentences with the correct words.

  1 In _____ photo, we're playing in the park.
  2 This photo is _____ my friend George.
  3 _____ is a photo of my teacher, Joanna.
  4 _____ this photo, we're having lunch.
  5 Here's _____ photo of London.
  6 This photo _____ of the other students in my class.

4 You are at a sports camp. Write an e-mail to a friend. Use personal pronouns to avoid repeating words and names.

Talk about:
- the weather
- your daily routine
- some photos and what you are doing in them.

4 REVIEW and PRACTICE

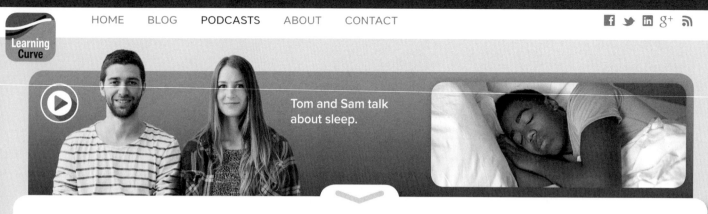

LISTENING

1 ▶ 4.5 Listen to the podcast about sleep. Check (✓) the things Dr. Patel talks about.

a using a computer ____
b lunch ____
c doing yoga ____
d teenagers ____
e taking a bath ____
f taking a shower ____
g watching TV ____
h breakfast ____

2 ▶ 4.5 Listen again. Does Dr. Patel say the things below? Choose Yes or No.

1	Most teenagers don't get enough sleep.	Yes	No
2	Most teenagers need eight hours sleep a night.	Yes	No
3	Dr. Patel eats a big lunch.	Yes	No
4	Dr. Patel has dinner late at night.	Yes	No
5	He takes a bath every evening.	Yes	No
6	He goes to bed after eleven o'clock.	Yes	No
7	He only works on his computer until six o'clock.	Yes	No
8	The light from your phone can stop you from relaxing.	Yes	No

READING

1 Read the blog on page 25 about the weather in two different countries. Match headings 1–5 with paragraphs A–E.

1 Different weather, different clothes ____
2 Making new friends in a new country ____
3 Sports at home and away ____
4 Different lives in two countries ____
5 Summer and winter weather ____

2 Check (✓) the true sentences.

1 Patrice is a student from Canada. ____
2 In Australia, you can swim in the sea in January. ____
3 He thinks life in Australia is similar to life in Canada. ____
4 He's wearing warm clothes today. ____
5 He hates the winter in Canada. ____
6 The weather in Canada is very different in the summer and winter. ____
7 Patrice doesn't have many friends in Australia. ____
8 He never goes surfing in Canada. ____

3 Circle the weather and seasons vocabulary in the blog.

24

REVIEW and PRACTICE 4

HOME BLOG PODCASTS ABOUT CONTACT

Guest blogger Marc writes about the weather in different countries.

NORTH AND SOUTH

What's the weather like in your country? Do you think the weather changes how you feel? What happens when people move from a hot country to a cold country, or from a cold place to somewhere really hot? Twenty-year-old Patrice Chiffre told me about moving from Canada to Australia.

A I come from Calgary, a city in Canada, but now I'm going to college in Australia. The weather in these countries isn't the same at all! And I think it changes how people live and work in these places.

C Where I'm living in Australia right now, there is a wet season and a dry season. The wet season is really hot, and the dry season is a little colder. But at home in Canada, the winters are long, dark, and really cold. The short and sunny summers bring a big change, so people often eat healthier food, get more exercise, and get up early in the morning. I love the summers in Canada – they are full of energy, festivals, and parties!

D People spend a lot of time outside in Australia, so it's easy to meet people and make new friends. Of course, it's different in Canada, especially in winter. People stay inside more and don't see their friends very often. I'm meeting lots of new people here in Australia!

B First, the months and seasons aren't the same. In December in Canada, people wear warm coats and hats, and sometimes have dinner next to a big fire. But in Australia, January is summer and July is winter. Today is the beginning of February, and everyone is wearing T-shirts and shorts. I'm eating lunch by the sea with my friends, and we're enjoying the sunny weather! People often spend New Year's at the beach here.

E One thing I love about Canada is all the snow and ice we have in winter. I love going skiing, too. It hardly ever snows here in Australia, but I enjoy going surfing – that's something I can't do at home!

25

UNIT 5

What are you wearing?

5A LANGUAGE

GRAMMAR: Simple present and present continuous

1 Choose the correct options to complete the sentences.

1 Ramona is Spanish. She *is coming from* / *comes from* Spain.
2 My aunt *doesn't work* / *isn't working* near her home.
3 *I eat* / *I'm eating* a big breakfast every morning.
4 "Where is Katia?" "There she is. *She's wearing* / *She wears* a blue jacket."
5 Hello! *Are you looking* / *Do you look* for me?
6 We *don't visit* / *aren't visiting* our grandparents very often.
7 *Is he watching* / *Does he watch* TV right now?
8 They *aren't selling* / *don't sell* magazines in this store.

2 Complete the conversation with the simple present or present continuous form of the verbs in parentheses.

Andy Hi! I'm Andy. ¹_____ (you/have) a good time?
Mara Yes, it's a great party! My name's Mara.
Andy Hi Mara! Where ²_____ (you/come from)?
Mara I'm from Brazil, but I ³_____ (study) in here in Chicago this summer. What about you?
Andy I'm from Boston, but I ⁴_____ (not live) there right now. I ⁵_____ (work) here with my parents for a few months.
Mara That's interesting! What ⁶_____ (they/do)?
Andy They ⁷_____ (fix) cars. We ⁸_____ (not make) a lot of money, but my mom ⁹_____ (enjoy) working with the family!
Mara That's fantastic! My mom ¹⁰_____ (not have) a job right now, but she wants to be a singer!

VOCABULARY: Clothes and ordinal numbers

3 Match definitions 1–8 with clothes a–h.

1 You might wear these on your legs at the beach. ____
2 This makes your neck warm on a cold day. ____
3 You can put these on your hands when it's cold. ____
4 Men often wear this at work. ____
5 You need these on your feet in the snow. ____
6 You can wear this on your head in summer or winter. ____
7 You wear this around the top of your pants. ____
8 When it's hot and sunny, people wear these on their feet. ____

a sandals
b belt
c hat
d gloves
e scarf
f shorts
g tie
h boots

4 Write the words next to the ordinal numbers.

1 11th _____
2 3rd _____
3 12th _____
4 29th _____
5 40th _____
6 36th _____
7 28th _____
8 19th _____
9 31st _____
10 14th _____

PRONUNCIATION: Dates

5 ▶5.1 Underline the stressed words. Listen, check, and repeat.

1 It's May fifteenth.
2 It's December sixth.
3 It's the thirtieth of November.
4 It's April eleventh.
5 It's October twelfth.
6 It's the twenty-third of June.
7 It's the sixteenth of February.
8 It's July twenty-ninth.
9 It's the fourteenth of January.
10 It's August thirty-first.

26

SKILLS 5B

READING: Identifying facts and opinions

ALL ABOUT CLOTHES ...

I'm Marta, and I'm a fashion blogger from Chile. I love making my own clothes and posting pictures of them on this blog!

A I write my blog at home. I need to wear warm clothes because my house is cold. In this picture, I'm wearing my favorite work clothes – I call this my uniform! I think this dress is [1]*anfcitsat* – it's really long, and it keeps me warm, too. My best friend makes jewelry – in this picture, I'm wearing one of her necklaces.

B I love walking, and there are lots of mountains in Chile. I often go hiking on the weekend. Here I am in my favorite hat and hiking pants. I think they're [2]*tearg*!

C I'm not just a fashion blogger! I also have a part-time job. I work as a waitress in a café near my home. I can wear what I like because there's no uniform. I usually wear this black skirt and attractive white top because I think it looks really [3]*cnei*. Do you like my shoes?

D This is my [4]*eautfilub* little brother! He's only five years old. I really like making clothes for him. He's wearing green pants and a T-shirt because these are his favorite clothes.

E The clothes I make aren't always good. This dress is horrible – it's [5]*sranibregams*! It's too big for me, and it's also too short. It's [6]*fulwa*, I know, but everyone makes mistakes!

1

2

3

4

5

1 Read Marta's blog. Match paragraphs A–E with pictures 1–5.

A ____
B ____
C ____
D ____
E ____

2 Order the letters in words 1–6 in the blog to make adjectives.

1 _____
2 _____
3 _____
4 _____
5 _____
6 _____

3 Read the sentences from some of Marta's other blog posts. Are they opinion (O) or fact (F)?

1 Shopping for clothes is boring. ____
2 There are 25 clothing stores in my town. ____
3 I think that my big brother's clothes are terrible! ____
4 My birthday is on June 23rd. I want to get some new shoes! ____
5 I don't have very nice clothes. ____
6 My mother is a nurse. ____

5C LANGUAGE

GRAMMAR: *Can* and *can't*

1 Complete the sentences with *can* or *can't*.

1 I _____ see it because I'm not wearing my glasses.
2 "_____ you help me, please?" "Yes, of course!"
3 "Where is the nearest café?" "I'm sorry, we're not from here. We _____ tell you."
4 Anita is a great photographer. She _____ take really good photos.
5 "Can Miguel cook Chinese food?" "No, he _____."
6 "_____ they speak French?" "Yes, a little."
7 Are you hungry? You _____ have some of my pizza if you want.
8 You _____ buy this book, but you can download it.
9 "Can you see the sea from your house?" "Yes, we _____."
10 She can go to the club tonight, but she _____ stay too late.

2 Complete the sentences with *can* or *can't* and the verbs in the box.

| run | read | teach | come | play | go out |
| hear | understand | ask | borrow |

1 "_____ I _____ you a question?" "Yes, what is it?"
2 Sarah _____ _____ soccer, but she likes watching it.
3 I'm going to Italy next week. _____ you _____ me some Italian words?
4 "Can you _____ this letter?" "No, I _____. The writing is really small."
5 I _____ _____ very fast because I'm wearing sandals!
6 Alina has a lot of homework, so she _____ _____ tonight.
7 _____ I _____ your book? It looks really interesting.
8 They _____ _____ to my party on Saturday – they're on vacation.
9 "Can you _____ that noise? "Yes, I _____ – what is it?"
10 I _____ _____ you – you're speaking too fast.

VOCABULARY: Hobbies

3 Match the two parts of the sentences.

1 My friend Anita makes ____
2 Our grandmother collects ____
3 His English teacher plays ____
4 Her sister takes ____
5 What does he draw ____
6 Can you bake ____

a pictures of?
b really good photos of animals.
c a cake for my birthday?
d jewelry like bracelets and necklaces.
e coins. She has over a thousand!
f the drums in a band.

4 Complete the sentences with the correct verbs.

1 At school, we _____ blogs about what we are learning.
2 Daniel _____ pictures of his girlfriend in beautiful colors.
3 My sister _____ online games for hours.
4 Can you _____ chess? Do you want to learn?
5 Costa's aunt wants to _____ him a sweater for the winter.
6 Not many people _____ stamps these days.

PRONUNCIATION: *Can* and *can't*

5 ▶ 5.2 Say the sentences. How do we say *can* and *can't*? Listen, check, and repeat.

1 I can't sew clothes. Can you?
2 "Can you speak Chinese?" "Yes, I can."
3 John can't sing, but he can play the drums.
4 My mom can cook really well.
5 I can dance, but I can't sing.
6 My dad can leave work early this week.
7 "Can your brother play the violin?" "No, he can't."
8 You can't buy a new top today.

SKILLS 5D

SPEAKING: Offering help

1 ▶5.3 Listen to Tim talking about shopping for his vacation. Check (✓) the clothes you hear.

a coat ___
b boots ___
c scarf ___
d shirt ___
e gloves ___
f sweater ___
g sandals ___
h shorts ___
i socks ___
j T-shirt ___

2 Complete the questions with the words in the box. Then match them with answers a–f below.

| sell | in | colors | pay | changing | much |

1 Do you have it _____ blue? ___
2 Do you _____ scarves? ___
3 What _____ are there? ___
4 How _____ is this green one? ___
5 Where are the men's _____ rooms, please? ___
6 Can I _____ with this credit card? ___

a They're all 45 dollars.
b I'll show you.
c We do, yes.
d Just a minute, I'll check. Yes, here you are.
e Certainly, sir.
f We have these in black, red, and green.

3 ▶5.3 Listen and check.

4 ▶5.4 Listen to 5 conversations. What does the salesclerk do? Choose the correct option.

	asks if the customer needs help	says that he/she will do something
1		
2		
3		
4		
5		

5 ▶5.4 Read the conversations. What do you think the salesclerk says? Then listen again and check.

1
Salesclerk Are you OK? Do you _____ any help?
Customer   Yes – do you sell coats?

2
Salesclerk Can I help _____?
Customer   Yes, please. How much are these pajamas?

3
Customer   Can I pay with this credit card?
Salesclerk Just a minute, I'll _____.

4
Customer   Where are the men's changing rooms?
Salesclerk I'll _____ you where they are.

5
Customer   Do you have this suit in medium?
Salesclerk _____ me ask someone.

6 ▶5.4 Listen again. Repeat what the salesclerk says.

29

5 REVIEW and PRACTICE

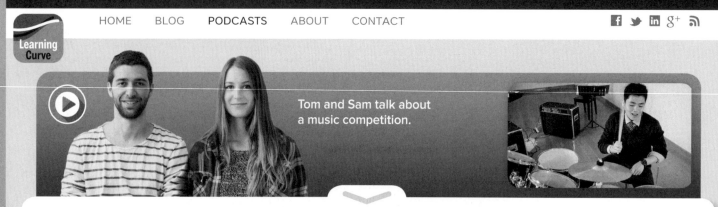

LISTENING

1 ▶ 5.5 Listen to the podcast about a music competition. Choose the correct answers.

1 How old is Tony Pia?
   a 17
   b 18
   c 20

2 What instrument can Tony play well?
   a the drums
   b the piano
   c the guitar

3 When is the final for the music competition?
   a June 30th
   b January 30th
   c June 13th

2 ▶ 5.5 Listen again. Complete the sentences with one or two words.

1 The competition is called Young Drummer of _____.
2 Young people from all over _____ enter the competition.
3 Tony is feeling a bit _____.
4 Tony's mom can play the _____.
5 Tony plays the drums every _____.
6 Playing the drums makes Tony feel _____ and full of energy.

READING

1 Read the blog on page 31 about what to wear for a job interview. Answer the questions.

1 What is Angela Santo's job?
2 What is Norbert Szil's job?
3 Which person's clothes does Angela prefer?
4 Which person's clothes does Norbert prefer?

2 Are the sentences correct? Choose Yes or No.

1	Angela and Norbert like Jo's hat.	Yes	No
2	Angela doesn't like Jo's scarf.	Yes	No
3	Norbert likes Jo's scarf and top.	Yes	No
4	Norbert thinks Dan looks good.	Yes	No
5	Angela thinks Dan is wearing great clothes for an interview.	Yes	No
6	Angela likes all Isa's clothes.	Yes	No
7	Angela thinks skirts are better than pants for an interview.	Yes	No
8	Norbert thinks Isa's clothes are good for a job in fashion.	Yes	No

3 Circle the clothes vocabulary in the blog.

REVIEW and PRACTICE 5

HOME **BLOG** PODCASTS ABOUT CONTACT

Guest blogger Ethan hears about wearing the right clothes.

Dress for success

You have an interview for the job of your dreams. Congratulations! So, what are you thinking of wearing on the big day? It can be easy to make bad choices. Angela Santo is a hotel manager, and Norbert Szil has a fashion business. They tell me how to dress for success.

Jo

Angela I'm not at all sure about this one. Why is she wearing a hat? I don't think that hats are a great idea – not for a job interview. And I don't think the scarf is very neat. It looks a little informal, too.

Norbert I agree with Angela about the hat. I don't agree with her about the rest of the clothes, though. This woman is wearing very fashionable clothes, and I think the scarf and top look good together. She looks cool!

Dan

Norbert This man is carrying an old briefcase. It's not at all attractive! It looks awful! I think he's wearing a suit, shirt, and tie, but are those sneakers on his feet? This is never a good look, but for a job interview it's terrible!

Angela I agree with Norbert. This man does not look fashionable. Are you sure he's going to a job interview?

Isa

Angela This woman has it right! The skirt is great – not too long or short – and it's dark blue, which is a great color for interviews. She's wearing a nice jacket, too. Suits are great for interviews, and women can wear pant suits or a skirt and jacket.

Norbert Is this woman looking for a job in a bank? I think she'll do well. There's just one thing – I can't imagine her working in fashion. Her clothes are a bit boring. Some color is always a great thing, and how about some jewelry?

31

UNIT 6 Homes and cities

6A LANGUAGE

GRAMMAR: there is/there are, some/any and prepositions of place

1 Complete the text with the words in the box.

there are	are	are there	there's
is	any	there	some

So, this is my bedroom – I really like it!
¹_____ a window by my bed, so I can see outside. Across from the bed is a TV. I love watching TV in bed at night! ²_____ some closets, too, for my clothes. ³_____ any shelves? Yes, there ⁴_____ – look! There are ⁵_____ shelves next to the bed. There aren't ⁶_____ books on them because I don't like reading. ⁷_____ are lots of DVDs, though. And ⁸_____ there a desk? No, I do my homework downstairs on the big table!

2 Choose the preposition which is **not** correct.

1 The boy is *in front of / behind / between* the door.
2 The table is *next to / across from / in* a small window.
3 The big chair is *on / behind / in front of* the closet.
4 Is his book *under / between / next to* your shopping bag?
5 My house is *between / under / across from* the park and the station.
6 Two apples are *in / under / on* the table.
7 Your cat is *behind / on / between* the sofa.
8 Is your apartment *next to / between / on* those two stores?
9 Our teacher is *in / next to / in front of* the big desk.
10 Her phone is *behind / in / under* the TV.

VOCABULARY: Rooms and furniture

3 Order the letters to make words for rooms or furniture.

1 Is there a TCLSEO in your bedroom?
_____
2 There are a lot of old books and toys in the TENSMEAB of our house.
_____
3 When it's sunny, I like sitting outside on the YLBCAON.
_____
4 We have got a AGGARE where my parents keep their car.
_____
5 Julia's in the THRABOMO. She's taking a shower.
_____
6 Their house has a OMORDEB upstairs, and one downstairs.
_____

4 Write the words for the definitions.

1 You look at your face in this.
m_____
2 You can wash your clothes in this.
w_____ m_____
3 This is a room at the top of a house.
a_____
4 You walk up and down these.
s_____
5 You eat food here.
d_____ r_____
6 There's grass and sometimes flowers and trees here.
b_____
7 You can do your homework here.
s_____
8 You cook food here.
k_____

PRONUNCIATION: there's/there are

5 ▶6.1 Say the sentences. How do we say *there's* and *there are*? Listen again and repeat.

1 There's a bed in the living room.
2 There are some chairs next to the table.
3 Is there a sofa in your bedroom?
4 Are there any shelves? No, there aren't.
5 There are five tables in their house.
6 Is there any food in the cabinet?
7 There's a stove in the kitchen.
8 There's no hall in his apartment.

SKILLS 6B

LISTENING: Identifying key points

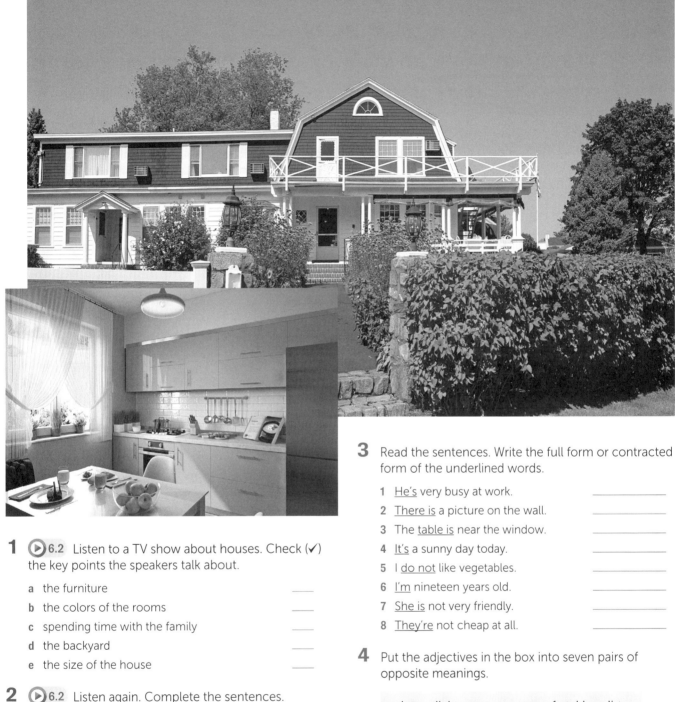

1 ▶ 6.2 Listen to a TV show about houses. Check (✓) the key points the speakers talk about.

a the furniture ____
b the colors of the rooms ____
c spending time with the family ____
d the backyard ____
e the size of the house ____

2 ▶ 6.2 Listen again. Complete the sentences.

1 The windows are really big and _____.
2 At first, the house had two _____.
3 Loretta has _____ children.
4 The host thinks their furniture is really _____.
5 Loretta's husband really likes _____ furniture.
6 Loretta painted the bathroom and _____.
7 The furniture was _____ expensive.
8 Loretta loves sitting on the _____ in the summer.

3 Read the sentences. Write the full form or contracted form of the underlined words.

1 He's very busy at work. _____
2 There is a picture on the wall. _____
3 The table is near the window. _____
4 It's a sunny day today. _____
5 I do not like vegetables. _____
6 I'm nineteen years old. _____
7 She is not very friendly. _____
8 They're not cheap at all. _____

4 Put the adjectives in the box into seven pairs of opposite meanings.

clean   light   narrow   uncomfortable   dirty
cheap   modern   quiet   heavy   expensive
traditional   wide   noisy   comfortable

1 _____ _____
2 _____ _____
3 _____ _____
4 _____ _____
5 _____ _____
6 _____ _____
7 _____ _____

33

6C LANGUAGE

GRAMMAR: Modifiers

1 Choose the correct options to complete the sentences.

1 I love Suzy's house! It's ____ beautiful.
   a pretty   b really   c not very
2 I don't like that dress – it's ____ attractive.
   a pretty   b not at all   c very
3 "Do you like this music?" "It's ____ good, but it's not my favorite."
   a not very   b not at all   c pretty
4 We don't want any dinner, thanks. We're ____ hungry.
   a really   b not very   c very
5 Everyone likes Laura. She's ____ friendly.
   a not very   b really   c pretty
6 "Can you clean your bedroom? It's ____ messy."
   a not at all   b not very   c really
7 "Can they speak English well?" "They can speak it ____ well, but they want to get better."
   a very   b not at all   c pretty
8 She's ____ good at sports. She often wins competitions!
   a not at all   b not very   c very

2 Order the words to make sentences.

1 sunny / not / today / it's / very
   _____
2 pretty / good student / is / Emile / a
   _____
3 really / costumes / your / colorful / are
   _____
4 friendly / her uncle / very / is / not
   _____
5 goes / early / to bed / Paola / very
   _____
6 not / my / warm / are / gloves / very
   _____

VOCABULARY: Places in a city

3 Order the letters to make words for places in a city.

1 QUESOM
   _____
2 TREHEAT
   _____
3 METNUNOM
   _____
4 HETACLADR
   _____
5 QERUAS
   _____
6 TRAPATEMN DIGLIBUN
   _____
7 RGEBID
   _____
8 NORETCC LALH
   _____

4 Complete the words.

1 My mom goes to the m_____t every morning to buy fruit and vegetables.
2 We live in an old city, so there aren't many s_____s or other tall buildings.
3 My sister loves reading. She's always at the l_____y.
4 There's a small s_____m here. There's a basketball game every weekend.
5 His brother-in-law's an accountant. He works in an o_____e b_____g.
6 In my village, there's a b_____e over the river.

PRONUNCIATION: Sentence stress

5 ▶ 6.3 Underline the stressed words in the sentences. Listen, check, and repeat.

1 That chair's not very comfortable.
2 Her grandparents' house is pretty modern.
3 It's a very famous painting.
4 That restaurant's not at all expensive.
5 Our balcony is always really sunny.
6 This is a pretty heavy table.
7 The restaurant is very traditional.

Skills 6D

WRITING: Topic sentences

A. _____ It's on the River Guadalquivir, but it's pretty far from the sea. It's a busy and lively place with a population of 700,000.

B. _____ You can visit museums, art centers, theaters, and movie theaters. The Plaza de España is a very famous place. It was built in 1928 and is really popular with tourists. If you like being active, you can play soccer or golf at the parks and sports centers. There are lots of great places to go walking, too.

C. _____ There are really fantastic restaurants where you can get delicious tapas and traditional Spanish food. You have to try the delicious potato omelet – it's fantastic!

D. _____ A lot of tourists come to the April Fair every spring. This celebration takes place next to the river – it's a wonderful party. There is horseback riding, music, and women wearing colorful flamenco dresses.

E. _____ Nicer times to visit are spring and fall, when it's sunny and a little bit cooler.

1 Read the text about Seville. Match paragraphs A–E with topic sentences 1–5.

1. If you visit Seville in the summer, it can be very hot. ___
2. Seville is also well known for its festivals. ___
3. You can always find something good to eat in this city. ___
4. Seville is a famous Spanish city. ___
5. There are so many things for tourists to see and do in Seville. ___

2 Complete each sentence about Rome with one word.

1. Rome is the _____ city of Italy.
2. More than 2.5 million people _____ there.
3. Walking is a great _____ to see the sights.
4. There are wonderful _____ of the city from the top of the Gianicolo hill.
5. If _____ like historic sights, go to the Colosseum.
6. There are also lots of really good _____ to eat.

3 Write about a city you know well. Begin each paragraph with a topic sentence. Include the following information:

Paragraph 1: Where is the city?
Paragraph 2: What can you do there?
Paragraph 3: What special events or festivals are there?
Paragraph 4: Where can you go to eat?
Paragraph 5: When is the best time to visit?

35

6 REVIEW and PRACTICE

HOME   BLOG   PODCASTS   ABOUT   CONTACT

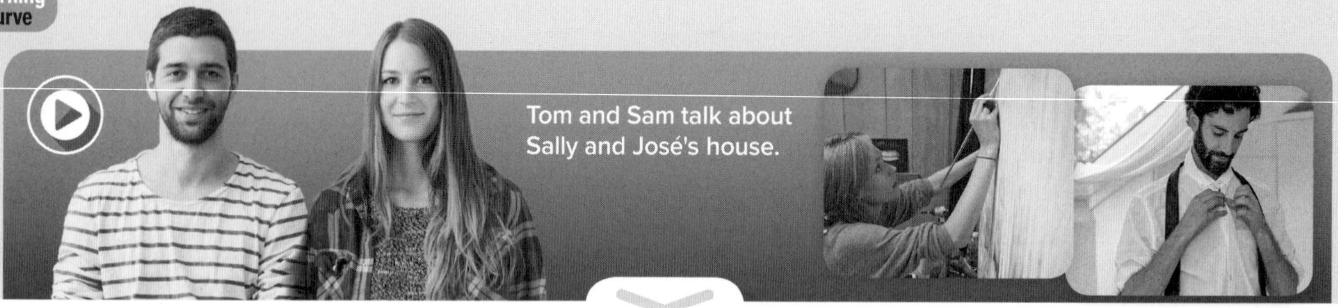

Tom and Sam talk about Sally and José's house.

LISTENING

1 🔊 6.4 Listen to the podcast about Sally and José's house. What is unusual about it?

a There is no furniture.
b There are two houses inside it.
c It's not very neat.

2 🔊 6.4 Listen again. Are the sentences true (T) or false (F)?

1 Sally and José live in the country. ___
2 They don't like each other. ___
3 They can't live together. ___
4 Sally goes to bed late. ___
5 José gets up early. ___
6 They are both clean and tidy. ___
7 They have the same rooms. ___
8 José doesn't see Sally every day. ___

3 🔊 6.4 Listen again and check (✓) the parts of the house that Sally and José mention.

1 backyard ___
2 dining room ___
3 kitchen ___
4 living room ___
5 bedroom ___
6 bathroom ___
7 basement ___
8 hall ___

READING

1 Read the blog on page 37 about Buenos Aires. Match paragraphs A–E with pictures 1–5.

1 ___
2 ___
3 ___
4 ___
5 ___

2 Choose the correct options to complete the sentences.

1 El Ateneo Grand Splendid doesn't sell
   a books.
   b furniture.
   c food and drink.
2 You can watch sports at
   a San Telmo.
   b La Poesía.
   c La Bombonera.
3 You don't have to pay for
   a the soccer games.
   b the walking tours.
   c the coffee at La Poesía.
4 They sell cheap clothes
   a in the park.
   b next to the theater.
   c at the market.
5 San Telmo has lots of
   a interesting buildings.
   b good places for music.
   c parks.
6 The street art tour
   a is in one part of the city.
   b is in different parts of the city.
   c starts next to an ice cream shop.

36

REVIEW and PRACTICE 6

HOME   BLOG   PODCASTS   ABOUT   CONTACT

Tom and Sam write about Buenos Aires.

The best of Buenos Aires

We asked our readers to tell us about their favorite places in the beautiful city of Buenos Aires. Thanks for all your great ideas. We want to go there – now! We hope you do, too, when you read our blog!

A   El Ateneo Grand Splendid
El Ateneo Grand Splendid is the best bookshop in the world! It's in a beautiful building, which is nearly a hundred years old. There are lots of books, balconies, and comfortable chairs, and there's a café that sells excellent coffee and delicious pastries. It's perfect for book lovers!

B   La Bombonera
Above the houses and stores of La Boca, you can find the soccer stadium. This is where the Boca junior soccer team plays. It's not too expensive to get a ticket for a game, and it's a really exciting place to spend some time.

C   City walking tours
Every day there are free walking tours of Buenos Aires, and you can choose to see the city during the day or at night. You'll visit modern and traditional buildings, from libraries to cathedrals. There is also a stop at the local market where you can buy clothes and food – clothes are not at all expensive here. The tour begins at the park across from the National Theater and finishes at a bar where you can hear some live Argentinian music.

D   San Telmo
San Telmo is the oldest part of the city. There are narrow streets full of interesting stores, monuments, and some excellent restaurants, too. It's a great place to find an outdoor café, order coffee, and watch the world go by. A very popular café is La Poesía. It's next to a beautiful old church.

E   Street art tour
Buenos Aires is famous for street art, and there are some really colorful paintings. The street art tour is a good way to learn about the artists in this amazing place. It takes you all over the city and finishes in a famous ice cream shop. The guides are really friendly, too!

Our next blog post is about Egypt. Do you have any useful travel tips? Let us know!

WRITING PRACTICE

WRITING: Opening and closing an informal e-mail

Hello Bella,

How are you? I hope everything's OK in Italy.

It's nice to meet you. My name's Andreas, and I'm eighteen years old. I'm from Germany, but I'm in the U.S. right now. I'm studying English at a language school. It's great here, but I don't like the weather – it's very hot!

I speak English every day with my host family. My host mother is a doctor, and she doesn't have a lot of free time. She has two sons: Andy and Greg. Greg is eighteen, and Andy is sixteen. They are both students.

On the weekend, we go shopping, or we play sports. Sometimes we go to the movies – there are some really good movie theaters here.

Write soon!

Andreas

1 Read Andreas's e-mail to a penpal. Complete the sentences.

1 Andreas is from _____.
2 He is eighteen _____ old.
3 Right now, Andreas is in _____.
4 He _____ the weather there.
5 He _____ sports on weekends.

2 Complete the sentences with *and*, *but*, or *or*.

1 Andreas is German, _____ he's eighteen.
2 Andreas can speak German _____ English.
3 He's from Germany, _____ now he is in the U.S.
4 He likes the U.S., _____ the weather is too hot.
5 He plays sports _____ he goes shopping on the weekend.

3 Are the words and phrases for opening (O) or closing (C) an informal e-mail?

1 Hi   O C
2 See you soon   O C
3 Hey   O C
4 Take care   O C
5 Hello   O C
6 Write soon   O C

4 Write an e-mail to a new friend.

- introduce yourself
- say your name, age, and where you live
- use informal language to open and close your e-mail

WRITING PRACTICE

WRITING: Describing a photo

Hi Malu,

How are you? How's your new job?

I know you like movies, so I'm sending you some photos of me with my movie club. We make movies together on Tuesday and Friday evenings, and we have a lot of fun. We sometimes go to the movies, too!

Here's a photo of us at the movie theater – we're watching a horror movie! The second photo is of Ella and Sam. They're making a movie in the park – it's a comedy, so they're laughing. Sam is holding the camera in his hand. He makes great movies.

See you soon,

Viktor

1 Read Viktor's e-mail. In what order (1–4) does he do things a–d?

  a talk about the movie club _____
  b close the e-mail _____
  c describe some photos of the movie club _____
  d open the e-mail _____

2 Viktor has some more photos of the movie club. Match the two parts of the sentences.

  1 In this photo, I'm with _____
  2 Here's a photo of Ella _____
  3 Here's a photo of _____
  4 In this photo, we're _____

  a and Sam with their cameras.
  b my friend, Bruce.
  c sitting in the movie theater together.
  d my favorite camera.

3 Complete the sentences with the personal pronouns in the box.

> I   you   he   she   it   we   they

  1 This is where the movie club meets. _____'s a small café near our college.
  2 Ella works part time. _____'s a waitress in a café.
  3 Ella and Sam sing and make music. _____'re really good actors, too.
  4 I'm with Sam. _____'re talking about ideas for our next movie.
  5 Sam has an older brother. _____'s in film school.
  6 What do you and your friends like doing? Do _____ enjoy watching movies?
  7 This is my camera. _____ love making movies with it!

4 Write an e-mail to a friend about a free-time activity you enjoy. Use the notes to help you plan your e-mail.

  Paragraph 1: Ask your friend how he/she is.
  Paragraph 2: Say what the activity is and why you like it.
  Paragraph 3: Say when you do it and with who.
  Paragraph 4: Describe two or three photos of your activity.

WRITING PRACTICE

WRITING: Topic sentences

Where to buy clothes in Paris

A _____ But where can you go to get the best clothes? It's easy when you know the city. Here are some of my favorite places.

B _____ There are lots of them in many parts of the city and you can find really interesting things. You can buy costumes and jewelry from the 1960s and 1970s – they're cheap, too.

C _____ On the Champs Élysées, there are lots of small stores. You can buy beautiful shirts, pants, and jackets. Movie stars and pop stars shop there, too!

D _____ The Centre Beaugrenelle is my favorite! It's a wonderful place to meet friends and go for coffee, too. You can also go to the movies there.

E _____ There are many great cafés and parks in Paris – you can always find somewhere to relax after shopping! Montmartre is a great area for restaurants!

1 Read the text about clothes shopping in Paris. Match topic sentences 1–6 with paragraphs A–E. There is one extra sentence.

1 If you like old clothes, go to the markets. _____
2 There are also a lot of big shopping centers. _____
3 The best time to go shopping in Paris is in the spring. _____
4 Shopping can be hard work sometimes. _____
5 Everyone knows that Paris is a fantastic place for clothes shopping. _____
6 There are also some very expensive stores in Paris. _____

2 Choose the correct options to complete the sentences.

1 There are lots _____ good places to go shopping in my city.
   a on   b of   c at
2 The City Mall is a good place _____ fashionable clothes.
   a in   b of   c for
3 There are wonderful views of the city _____ the top floor of this shopping center.
   a to   b from   c in
4 If you _____ to find some really different clothes, go to the Saturday market.
   a want   b try   c take
5 Eating at the View Café is a great _____ to finish the day after shopping.
   a time   b way   c part

3 Write a description of some different places to go shopping in your town or city. Begin each paragraph with a topic sentence.

Paragraph 1: Describe the locations.
Paragraph 2: Say what you can buy there.
Paragraph 3: Say the best time to visit them.
Paragraph 4: Say what you like about the places.

1 The story happened _____ week.

NOTES

NOTES

NOTES

Richmond

58 St Aldates
Oxford
OX1 1ST
United Kingdom

First reprint: July 2018
Printed in China
ISBN: 978-84-668-2553-5
© Richmond / Santillana Global S.L. 2017

All rights reserved. No part of this book may be reproduced, stored in a retrieval system or transmitted in any form by any means, electronic, mechanical, photocopying, recording, or otherwise, without the prior permission in writing of the Publisher.

Publishing Director: Deborah Tricker
Publisher: Simone Foster
Media Publisher: Sue Ashcroft
Workbook Publisher: Luke Baxter
Editors: Debra Emmett, Tom Hadland, Fiona Hunt, Eleanor Clements, Helen Wendholt
Americanization: Deborah Goldblatt, Jennifer Wise
Proofreaders: Peter Anderson, Shannon Neill, Fiona Hunt
Design Manager: Lorna Heaslip
Cover Design: This Ain't Rock'n'Roll, London
Design & Layout: Lorna Heaslip, Oliver Hutton, 320 Design, ColArt Design
Photo Researcher: Magdalena Mayo
Learning Curve **video:** Mannic Media
Audio production: Eastern Sky Studios
App development: The Distance

We would also like to thank the following people for their valuable contribution to writing and developing the material:
Graham Fruen, Bob McLarty, Brigit Viney, Pamela Vittorio (Video Script Writer), Belen Fernandez (App Project Manager), Rob Sved (App Content Creator)

Illustrators:
Simon Clare, Richard Duckett, James Gibbs and Olvind Hovland c/o NB Illustration; Dermot Flynn c/o Dutch Uncle; John Goodwin, Joanna Kerr c/o New Division; John Holcroft; Neal c/o KJA Artists

Photos:
Alicia García; B. Balaguer; C. Pérez; J. Jaime; S. Enríquez; S. Padura; V. Atmán; 123RF; A. G. E. FOTOSTOCK/Pixtal, Fancy; ABB FOTÓGRAFOS; ALAMY/New York City, Johner Images, Josef Polc, Ira Berger, eye35, Geraint Lewis, David Crausby, Peter Usbeck, Nikreates, Joe Vogan, Urbanmyth, AF archive, Cultura RM, Phililp Quirk, Philip Scalia, AGF Srl, Jozef Polc, Roman Babakin, peter dazeley, Hero Images Inc., CRIBER PHOTO, Jim West, studiomonde, Ian Shaw, Zoonar GmbH, Thomas Cockrem, Blend Images, Ian Francis stock, Image Source, Olaf Doering, Peter Schatz, ONOKY - Photononstop, Roger Bamber, Tetra Images, Vadym Drobot, Aurora Photos, B Christopher, Brendan Duffy, Chloe Johnson, Pablo Paul, Y.Levy, Steven May, Michael Dwyer, STOCKFOLIO®, age fotostock, D. Hurst, Milan Machaty, aberCPC, Minkimo, View Stock, robertharding, Kevin Britland, Juan Aunion, REUTERS, Jochen Tack, Keith Leighton, Jorge Tutor, Peter Forsberg, Radharc Images, Fredrick Kippe, Danita Delimont, Francis Specker, Joerg Boethling, Loop Images Ltd, Wavebreak Media, Bill Bachmann, David Kilpatrick, Dzianis Apolka, Jan Halaska, Perry van Munster, Bernardo Galmarini, Jose Luis Stephens, Andrey Kekyalyaynen, Homer Sykes archive, Konstantin Kalishko, Jonathan Smith, dpa picture alliance, Cultura Creative (RF), Jeff Greenberg 6 of 6, World History Archive, mauritius images GmbH, SIBSA Digital Pvt. Ltd., JTB Media Creation, INC., Henry Westheim Photography, Richard Wareham Fotografie, Sally and Richard Greenhill, The National Trust Photolibrary, epa european pressphoto agency b.v., Karol Kozlowski Premium RM Collection, Imagestate Media Partners Limited - Impact Photos, Universal Images Group North America LLC / DeAgostini, Magdalena Mayo; COMSTOCK; COVER; GETTY IMAGES SALES SPAIN/Erik Isakson/Tetra Images, Thinkstock/Jochen Sand, Toronto Star Archives, istock/Thinkstock, Adrian Weinbrecht, Photos.com Plus, TothGaborGyula, Paulo Fridman, Morsa Images, Alison Buck, stefanamer, Thinkstock, Jacobs Stock Photography, Bloomberg, Auscape; HIGHRES PRESS STOCK/AbleStock.com; I. PREYSLER; ISTOCKPHOTO/digitalskillet, sunstock, YvanDube, ImageGap, DarthArt, Getty Images Sales Spain; REX SHUTTERSTOCK/Max Lakner/BFA, Eugene Adebari, Tnt/BFA.com, Snap Stills, Howard/ANL; SETH POPPEL YEARBOOK LIBRARY; SHUTTERSTOCK/Sky Designs, Dean Drobot, Fotocrisis; STOCKBYTE; Jim Benjaminson Collections via the Plymouth Bulletin; Samsung; SERIDEC PHOTOIMAGENES CD; J. Lucas; M. Sánchez; Prats i Camps; 123RF; ALAMY/Blend Images, INTERFOTO, REUTERS, Keith Homan, MBI, imageBROKER, Jose Luis Suerte, Harold Smith, Ian Allenden, Peter Horree, MS Bretherton, Pulsar Images, andy lane, Nano Calvo, Radharc Images, Westend61 GmbH, Colin Underhill, Gianni Muratore, Mary Evans Picture Library, Michael Wheatley, Alibi Productions, a-plus image bank, ONOKY - Photononstop, Directphoto Collection, Arterra Picture Library, Martin Thomas Photography, Agencja Fotograficzna Caro, Cathy Topping, Blend Images - BUILT Content, Geraint Lewis; GETTY IMAGES SALES SPAIN/Thinkstock; I. PREYSLER; ISTOCKPHOTO/Getty Images Sales Spain; SHUTTERSTOCK; SHUTTERSTOCK NETHERLANDS,B.V.; SOUTHWEST NEWS/Leicester Mercury; ARCHIVO SANTILLANA

Cover Photo: istockphoto/wundervisuals

We would like to thank the following reviewers for their valuable feedback which has made Personal Best possible. We extend our thanks to the many teachers and students not mentioned here.
Brad Bawtinheimer, Manuel Hidalgo, Paulo Dantas, Diana Bermúdez, Laura Gutiérrez, Hardy Griffin, Angi Conti, Christopher Morabito, Hande Kokce, Jorge Lobato, Leonardo Mercato, Mercilinda Ortiz, Wendy López

The Publisher has made every effort to trace the owner of copyright material; however, the Publisher will correct any involuntary omission at the earliest opportunity.